John A. Bering, Thomas Montgomery

History of the Forty-Eighth Ohio Vet. Vol. Inf.

giving a complete account of the regiment from its organization at Camp Dennison,

O., in October, 1861, to the close of the war, and its final muster-out, May 10, 1866

John A. Bering, Thomas Montgomery

History of the Forty-Eighth Ohio Vet. Vol. Inf.

giving a complete account of the regiment from its organization at Camp Dennison, O., in October, 1861, to the close of the war, and its final muster-out, May 10, 1866

ISBN/EAN: 9783337267971

Printed in Europe, USA, Canada, Australia, Japan

Cover: Foto ©Andreas Hilbeck / pixelio.de

More available books at **www.hansebooks.com**

OF THE

FORTY-EIGHTH OHIO VET. VOL. INF.

Giving a Complete Account of the Regiment

FROM ITS ORGANIZATION AT CAMP DENNISON, O., IN
OCTOBER, 1861, TO THE CLOSE OF THE
WAR, AND ITS FINAL MUSTER-
OUT, MAY 10, 1866.

INCLUDING

All Its Marches, Camps, Battles, Battle-Scenes, Skirmishes, Sieges, Bivouacs, Picketing, Foraging and Scouting; With Its Capture, Prison Life and Exchange.

EMBRACING, ALSO,

AN ACCOUNT OF THE ESCAPE AND RE-CAPTURE OF
MAJOR J. A. BERING AND LIEUT. W. J. SROFE,
AND THE CLOSING EVENTS OF THE WAR
IN THE TRANS-MISSISSIPPI DEP'T.

BY
JOHN A. BERING,
Late Major 48th Ohio, and
THOMAS MONTGOMERY,
Late Captain 48th Ohio.

HILLSBORO, OHIO:
PRINTED AT THE HIGHLAND NEWS OFFICE.
1880.

TO THE MEMORY OF

OUR FALLEN COMRADES,

WHO DIED IN DEFENSE OF THEIR COUNTRY IN THE WAR
OF THE REBELLION, WHETHER THEY FELL UPON
THE BATTLE-FIELD OR WASTED AWAY FROM
WOUNDS AND DISEASE IN HOSPITALS
AND PRISONS; WHETHER THEY
LIE BURIED IN LONELY SOUTHERN
FIELDS OR RETURNED HOME TO SUFFER AND
SINK INTO UNTIMELY GRAVES, THIS VOLUME IS MOST

AFFECTIONATELY DEDICATED

BY THE AUTHORS.

PREFACE.

Our object, in writing the History of the Forty-eighth Ohio, was to preserve the record of a Regiment whose services, extending over a period of nearly five years, had gained for it the reputation of having done its whole duty, whether in camp, on the march, or in the trying hour of battle, as attested by its Brigade and Division Commanders.

We began arranging and compiling the material, consisting of our old army letters, diaries, company record, official reports, etc. etc., in 1870, and had it ready for the press in 1873; but owing to various causes we have delayed its publication until the present time.

We were both present with the Regiment, from the time we joined it at Camp Dennison, in October, 1861, until one made his escape from prison, in August, 1864, and the other, until mustered out in January, 1865; therefore we were eye-witnesses to, and participated in, the varied events narrated.

The record, from January, 1865, until the final

muster-out, May 10, 1866, was furnished principally by Lieut. James Douglas. We are also indebted to Lieut. W. J. Srofe for many items covering the same period.

In conclusion, we will say to the surviving members of the Regiment, that we do not claim any merit for this volume as a literary production. It is simply a narration of events, as seen by us, and was written at intervals, as the time could be spared from a busy life. Should it meet the approbation of our comrades, and be the means of perpetuating the deeds and memory of those who gave up their lives for the cause for which we fought, we will feel ourselves fully compensated for our labor. J. A. B. AND T. M.

LYNCHBURG, HIGHLAND Co., O.,
June, 1880.

CONTENTS.

HISTORY OF THE FORTY-EIGHTH OHIO.

CHAPTER I.
The Fall of Fort Sumpter — President's Call for Volunteers — Organization of a Company at Lynchburg — Recruiting at Camp Harvey — Muster-in at Webertown — Farewell Sermon. pp. 1—5

CHAPTER II.
Leaving Lynchburg — Arrival at Camp Dennison — Assigned to Quarters — Drill — Uniforms — Tents — Visits of Citizens of Lynchburg — Presentation of Swords — New Quarters — First Payment — Full Companies — Regiment Full — Field and Staff — Band — Monotony of Camp Life. pp. 6—11

CHAPTER III.
Marching Orders — Steamboat Ride Down the Ohio — Paducah — Without Arms — Rumors of an Attack — Armed with Austrian Rifles — Up the Tennessee — Fort Henry — Hog Mountain — First Shot — Savannah — Pittsburg Landing — Death of Capt. Ireland — Rebel Graves — Disembarking — First Camp. pp. 12—16

CHAPTER IV.
Camp at Shiloh Church — Reconnoisance — Lieut. Greer Captured — Orders for Strict Watch — Battle Imminent — The Attack of April 6th — Long-Roll — In Line of Battle — To the Support of the Pickets — Counter-March — Second Line of Battle — The Rebel Charge and Repulse — Arrival of Capt. Hammond — Orders to Retreat — New Position — Repulse of the Enemy —

Camp of the 81st Ohio — Arrival at the Landing — Advance to Support a Battery — The Rebel Charge — Their Repulse and Retreat — Arrival of Gen. Buell's Troops — Night — Rain.   pp. 17—24

CHAPTER V.

Battle of the Seventh — The Final Rout — Reoccupying Our Camps — The Battle-field — Burial of the Dead — Following the Enemy on the Eighth — The Attack on the 77th Ohio — The 48th Ohio to Their Support — Return to Camp — Our Dead and Wounded — Extracts from the Cincinnati Dailies — The Battle No Surprise — Loss in Both Armies — Extracts from Gen. Sherman's Official Report — Arrival of the Sanitary Commission — Gen. Halleck Takes Command — Band Discharged — Drill.   pp. 25—40

CHAPTER VI.

On the Road to Corinth — Order to March — Joke on Sergeant Reed — First Earthworks — Second Advance — Camp Number Six — Engagement at the Russell House — Talk with the Rebel Pickets — Separation of Mother and Child — Last Line of Earthworks — Evacuation of Corinth — The Pursuit and Return — Comparison of the Two Armies.   pp. 41—50

CHAPTER VII.

On to Memphis — Visit of Thomas Peale, Esq., of Lynchburg — Return of Lieut. Col. Parker — La-Grange — Moscow — Lafayette — Newton and the Snake — Return to Moscow — March to Holly Springs and Return — Contrabands — On the March to Memphis — White Station - Memphis — Camp at Fort Pickering — Maj. Wise and Lieut. Fields Resign — Return of Absentees — On Provost Guard — Cincinnati Reported Captured — Trip to Randolph — Rebel Cotton Burners.
   pp. 51—59

CHAPTER VIII.

Expedition for Vicksburg — Marching Orders — Down the Mississippi — Milliken's Bend — Up the Yazoo — March Through the Swamps — First Attack on Vicksburg — Picketing — Evacuation — Up the Mississippi and Arkansas Rivers — Arkansas Post — Battle and Capture of the Garrison — Loss in Killed and Wounded.
pp. 60—68

CHAPTER IX.

Return Down the River — Napoleon — Young's Point — Digging the Canal — Overflowed — Scheme Abandoned — Pioneer Corps — Promotions — Arrival of General Grant — New Camp — Milliken's Bend — Change of Surgeons — Paymaster — Complimentary Order — Major Moats — Military Board — Seventeenth Ohio Battery.
pp. 69—74

CHAPTER X.

Marching Orders — To the Rear of Vicksburg — Holmes' Plantation — Extract from General Sherman's "Memoirs" — Our Gun-boats Passing the Vicksburg Batteries — Smith's Landing — Return of Lieut. Col. Parker — Lake St. Joe — Grand Gulf — Crossing the Mississippi at Bruinsburg — Battle of Magnolia Hills — Port Gibson — Grind-Stone Ford — Foragers — Rocky Springs — Willow Springs — Cayuga — Gen. Sherman's Visit — Old Auburn — Raymond — Battle of Champion Hills — Black River Bridge. pp. 75—84

CHAPTER XI.

Assault on the Nineteenth — Attack on the Twentieth — Charge on the Twenty-Second — Our Flag on the Rebel Fort — Retreat After Night — Killed and Wounded — Extract from Cincinnati Commercial — Flag of Truce — Burying the Dead — Picketing and Mining — Blowing Up of Fort Hill — Surrender of Vicksburg, July 4th.
pp. 85—95

CHAPTER XII.

Marching Orders for Jackson — Excessive Heat — Siege of Jackson — Gen. Johnston Evacuates — Return to Vicksburg — Furloughs — Col. P. J. Sullivan Resigns — Steamer "City of Madison" Blown Up — Embarking for New Orleans — Camp at Carrollton — Grand Review by Gens. Grant and Banks — Extract from New Orleans Era. pp. 96—106

CHAPTER XIII.

Ordered to Western Louisiana — Berwick City — Teche Country — Franklin — Orange Groves — Election for Governor of Ohio — Guarding Steamers on the Teche — Surprise of the First Brigade — New Iberia — Foraging — Protection Papers. pp. 107—111

CHAPTER XIV.

Ordered to New Orleans — Embarking for Texas — Trip Across the Gulf — De Crow's Point — Dog-Tents — Distributing the Amnesty Proclamation — Planting the Flag in Texas — Skirmish Drill — Fishing and Gathering Shells — Short Rations — Cold New Year — Veterans — Ordered on Board a Condemned Vessel — Return to New Orleans — Re-enlisting — Veteran Medals — Promotions. pp. 112—125

CHAPTER XV.

Ordered to Franklin — Guarding Pontoon Train — Alexandria — Natchitoches — Capture of Pavy and McCune — Guarding the Wagon Train — Battle of Sabine Cross Roads — Out of Ammunition — Enemy in the Rear — Retreat Cut Off — Capture — On Our Way to Prison — Extracts from Gen. Ransom's Official Report — Number Captured — Extracts from Report of Committee on Conduct of the War — The Rebel General Taylor's Report of the Battle — First Night as Prisoners — Confederate Rations — School House — Marshall — Flag Song.
pp. 126—151

CHAPTER XVI.

Arrival at Camp Ford—The Stockade—Building Huts—Col. Allen Relieved by Col. Border—Adjutant McEachan—"Keno"—Tied Up by the Thumbs—Rations Cut Off—The Famous Order, "Kill All Recaptured Prisoners"—New Recruits from Gen. Steel's Army—Building Hospital—Poisonous Insects—Fourth of July Celebration—Exchange of One Thousand Prisoners—New "Cart-el"—Tunneling—Our Flag in Prison—Different Trades—Inflation Prices—Old Citizen Dumped—Brutal Treatment of Prisoners—Escape of Maj. Bering and Lieut. Srofe—New Commander.
pp. 152—170

CHAPTER XVII.

Paroled—Leaving Camp Ford—Arrival at Four-Mile Spring—Maj. Bering and Lieut. Srofe on Their Way Back to Prison—Journey to Grand Ecore—Camped at Alexandria—Arrival at the Mississippi—Exchanged—The Old Flag—New Orleans—Col. Dwight—Natchez—Provost Guard—Consolidated with the 83d Ohio—Home on Veteran Furlough. pp. 171—180

CHAPTER XVIII.

Preparation for Active Service Again—Brigaded with Colored Troops—Embarking for New Orleans—Arrival at Barrancas, Fla.—Prison Veterans Re-join from Furlough—Pascagoula—Ft. Blakely Invested—The Charge and Capture—Up the Alabama River—Selma—Return to Mobile—Explosion of Rebel Ammunition—Ordered to Texas — Arrival at Galveston — Muster-Out of the 83d Ohio—The Old 48th Ohio Itself Again—Ordered to Houston—Break-Bone Fever—Back to Galveston—Promotions—On Various Duties—Final Muster-Out—Arrival at Columbus—Home and a Quiet Life—Reid's History of the 48th Ohio—Testimonials of Brigade and Division Commanders. pp. 181—197

THE ESCAPE AND RE-CAPTURE

OF MAJ. J. A. BERING AND LIEUT. W. J. SROFE.

CHAPTER I.

Preparing Rations—The Forged Pass—Concealed in Sight of Prison—" Ten O'Clock and All's Well "—Crossing the Sabine River—Crossing the Bridge at the Mill—The Blood-Hounds on Our Trail—Run Into a Trap—Hounds Baffled—Escape—Man with a Gun—Passing Around a Village—An All Night Tramp—Moonlight View of the Country—Hounds on the Trail Again—Narrow Escape from the Hounds—Parching Corn Under Difficulties—Lost in a Dark Swamp—Waiting for the Moon to Rise. pp. 201—215

CHAPTER II.

Making a Raft—Crossing Little Cypress—Wading the Overflowed Bottoms—Crossing Big Cypress—Crossing Sulphur Fork—Wading and Swimming—Pass for a Rebel Deserter—Begging for Something to Eat—Relating Camp Rumors—Journey Interrupted by Rain—Capturing a Slave on a Mule—In the Indian Territory—Out of Our Course—Conversation with Three Slaves—The First Dinner—Carried Down the Stream—A Night Among the Owls and Mosquitos—Fording Little River. pp. 216—228

CHAPTER III.

The Arkansas Hills—The Hum of the Spinning-Wheel—The Last Match—Roast Pumpkin and Parched Corn—Almost Home—Re-Captured—Bound With Ropes—A Retrograde Movement—Another Unfortunate Yankee—On Exhibition—Entertained by Young Ladies—The Old Lady's Lecture on the War—Sent to Washington, Arkansas—The Guests in the Parlor—In the Court House—Offer of "Jewelry"—Rebel Officers on a Spree—On the Road to Camden—Battle-Field of Prairie d' Ann—Eating Two Days' Rations for Supper—Slaughter of the Colored Troops—No Quarter. pp. 229--240

CHAPTER IV.

In the Cotton-Shed at Camden—Pandemonium—Sent to the Hospital—On the Road Again—Guarded by Blood-Hounds—Prisoners Lassoed—Wading Through a Stream by Request—Arrival at Shreveport—Meeting Our Regiment Homeward Bound — Our First Mail—No Water for " Yankees"—Camp Ford—Home Again—Sentenced —Our New Cabin—Northers—Presidential Election—Tramping in the Ring. pp. 241—555

CHAPTER V.

The Rebel Army Ordered to Richmond, Va.—The Troops Refuse to Cross the Mississippi—Invasion of Missouri —Rebel Soldiers Plundering their Own People—Burial of the Beef—Plot to Overpower the Guards—1,200 Prisoners Exchanged—Their Condition When They Reached New Orleans—The Last Ditch—Foreign Intervention—Lee's Surrender—The War to Last Forty Years Longer—"The Gates Ajar"—The Homeward Journey—Under the Old Flag—Mustered Out— Description of Camp Ford, Three Months After our Departure—Destruction of Camp Ford. pp. 256—272

APPENDIX.

Additional List of Killed and Wounded of the 48th Ohio Vet. Vols.—List of Officers of the 13th Army Corps, Prisoners at Camp Ford, Texas—Roster of the Commissioned Officers of the 48th Ohio Vet. Vols.
pp. 273—284

ERRATUM.

On page 64, line 14, for 40,000 men, read 30,000.

HISTORY
OF THE
FORTY-EIGHTH OHIO
Veteran Volunteer Infantry.

CHAPTER I.

The Fall of Fort Sumpter — President's Call for Volunteers — Organization of a Company at Lynchburg — Recruiting at Camp Harvey — Muster-in at Webertown — Farewell Sermon.

THE memorable political campaign of 1860, that resulted in the election of Abraham Lincoln as President, was over. The Southern States, which had made threats of leaving the Union before his election, began to secede, one after another, and the whole country was in a state of feverish excitement.

No one seemed to be able to avert the coming storm. Thus matters stood, until that eventful day for us, as a nation, arrived. On the 12th day of April, 1861, Gen. Beauregard made the attack on Fort Sumpter, which, after a terrific bombardment of thirty-six hours, the garrison, under command of Maj. Anderson, was compelled to surrender to the Confederate forces.

When the startling news flashed over the wires, the whole North, from the "shores of Maine, to the Pacific Slope," arose in its might. Ignoring party lines, the people rallied under the immortal words of Gen. Jackson, "The Union — it must and shall be preserved." Then the President called for seventy-five thousand men, to serve three months, which many believed would settle the whole affair. But no sooner had the call been filled, and the troops sent to the front, than they were outnumbered by the seceding States at every point.

Another call was made by the President, this time for three hundred thousand volunteers, to serve three years, unless sooner discharged. Following the call came the reverse at Bull Run, which fell with stunning effect on the over-confident North. The whole effort of the Government was now concentrated on a vigorous prosecution of the war.

Up to this time volunteers had been leaving Lynchburg, Ohio, singly and in squads of three and four, to join the regiments then organizing in Camp Dennison, Ohio. A company of Home Guards had been organized in August; but no one had succeeded in raising a company for service in the field until John W. Frazee, who had been teaching a select school at Lynchburg, proposed to raise a company for active service, for one year, to be attached to the 60th Reg't. O. V. I., then organizing at Hillsboro, Ohio. He had no difficulty in collecting around him fifteen or twenty men, who formed the nucleus of what afterwards became Company C, 48th Reg't. O. V. I.

Sept. 20th, 1861, the company numbered twenty-seven men. An election of commissioned and non-commissioned officers was held in the schoolhouse at Lynchburg, which resulted in the election of J. W. Frazee, Captain; Peter Brown, 1st Lieut.; T. L. Fields, 2d Lieut.; Wm. A. Quarterman, 1st Sergt.; W. A. Pratt, J. A. Bering and Frank Holladay, Sergeants. After the election, the company, with two or three exceptions, decided to enlist for three years.

The company being in need of quarters, Mr. Josiah Harvey tendered us the use of his warehouse, which was accepted and named, "Camp Harvey."

Regular excursions were made by the company from the camp to the neighboring villages, where rousing war meetings were held, and sumptuous meals spread before the young soldiers, which generally resulted in getting new recruits. In the course of our travels we visited Dodsonville, Allensburg, Danville, Pricetown, McCarty's School-House, Fayetteville, and Webertown. At the latter place, on the 3d day of October, 1861, after a grand supper in Liggett's Grove, the company, numbering sixty men, was sworn into the United States service by Capt. J. W. Frazee, who had just returned from Columbus, with the proper authority. The company then returned to Camp Harvey, and soldiering, as we then considered it, began in earnest. We drilled twice a day, guards were posted, passes and furloughs issued, and strict discipline was enforced. And last, but not least, regular details for cooks were made each day. A two-horse wagon accompanied us on our trips, and hauled all surplus provisions to camp. Great credit is due the patriotic citizens of Lynchburg and vicinity, for their liberality in contributing to those grand dinners and suppers, and in furnishing Camp Harvey, free of all expense to the Government, the necessary supplies. The ladies, in particular, will be ever held in grateful remembrance, for their untiring efforts in contributing everything necessary to make us comfortable. Where all did so nobly for our common cause, it is difficult to particularize any one, but we cannot pass by the names of those that devoted their time and labor in organizing war meetings and making patriotic speeches., Foremost among them were Dr. S. J. Spees, Dr. R. Fulton, Rev. N. W. Cummins, Hon. A. D. Coombs, Isaac Robb, and many others. To such patriotic citizens was due, in a great measure, the promptness with which the company was recruited and sent to the field, while other companies were months in Camp Dennison before they were filled.

The company remained at Camp Harvey until Monday, Oct. 14th, when we were ordered to

Camp Dennison. The day preceding, the company assembled in the M. E. church, at 2 o'clock P. M., when Rev. Dr. Fulton preached our farewell sermon, to a large congregation. This was jestingly called our "funeral sermon," which, alas! proved too true to many. Of the twenty-three of the company that were killed, or who died from disease during the war, not one was ever known to have a sermon preached at his funeral.

CHAPTER II.

Leaving Lynchburg — Arrival at Camp Dennison — Assigned to Quarters — Drill — Uniforms — Tents — Visits of Citizens of Lynchburg — Presentation of Swords — New Quarters — First Payment — Full Companies — Regiment Full — Field and Staff — Band — Monotony of Camp Life.

IN the mean time, Capt. Frazee had been to Camp Dennison, and decided to attach his company to the 48th Regt. O. V. I., Col. Sullivan, commanding. Long before dawn on the 14th, the people of the surrounding country began to wend their way to Lynchburg, to witness the company's departure, which now numbered 82, officers and men. After parading through the principal streets, we halted in front of our camp, and took leave of our families and friends. The parting over, we boarded the cars, and were off to join our Regiment.

We arrived at Camp Dennison at 10 A. M. and were introduced to Colonel P. J. Sullivan, who welcomed us in a short, patriotic speech, after which we gave him three rousing cheers, and were marched to the quarters of Capt. Parker's company, from New Lexington, Highland county, Ohio, where we partook of our first meal, furnished by "Uncle Sam," which consisted of coffee, rice, potatoes, bacon and bread. Quite a change from Camp Harvey rations, of beefsteak, roast chicken, cakes, pies, preserves, &c., &c. After dinner we were examined by a regular Army Surgeon. Our previous examination had been made by Dr. S. J. Spees. The surgeon rejected R. B. Barnett, Peter Snider, William Stroup and John Aber; but they were finally accepted, and the majority of them proved as able for the service as many others, who passed the examination. We were then assigned to our quarters, consisting of frame shanties, ten by twelve feet, with room sufficient to accommodate twelve men. Each company had eight shanties, one kitchen, and a building for the officers.

We have given the history of the company, from its organization until it linked its fortunes with the 48th Ohio. And now we will trace the history of the Regiment, through the long and tedious years of the war.

The every day duty of the Regiment was squad, company and battalion drill, with dress parade in the evening, besides regular guard and fatigue duty. On Sundays, at 9 o'clock A. M., the companies were drawn up in a line, and inspected by their respective Captains. After the inspection the first Sergeants read the "Articles of War," in which nearly every other section ended, "Any violator of said section shall suffer *death*, or such other punishment as by a court martial shall be inflicted."

After inspection the companies were dismissed until 11 o'clock A. M. when they were marched to the Colonel's quarters, where a sermon was preached by the Chaplain. With dress-parade in the evening, the Sabbath day duties were closed, excepting for those on guard.

Oct. 20th, we received our suits of blue, and on the day following our tents, and were instructed in pitching and striking tents. Oct. 28th, the citizens of Lynchburg and vicinity sent a large delegation, with well-filled baskets, and three beautiful regulation swords, and presented them to Capt. Frazee, Lieutenants Brown and Fields, Hon. A. D. Coombs making the presentation address, which was pronounced by all who heard it, truly eloquent and very appropriate for the occasion. The officers responded, by pledging themselves never to betray the confidence reposed in them by their friends. Remarks were also made by Gen. M. S. Wade, Commanding Officer of Camp Dennison, and Col. Sullivan.

Nov. 8th, we moved out of the old shanties into tents, to enable the carpenters to remove them and build new quarters. We remained in the tents until the latter part of the month, when we took possession of our new buildings. They were large and comfortable; 100 feet long by 22 feet wide, with three tiers of bunks, the full length, on each side, capable of accommodating 98 men, with a large, commodious kitchen in the rear, and a separate building for the use of the commissioned officers of each company. Two large wood-stoves were furnished each building for heating purposes, making very comfortable quarters for the winter.

Jan. 15th, the Paymaster arrived, and paid our Regiment up to the first of January, which settled the oft-disputed question whether we would ever get any pay for our services. All under five dollars was paid in coin, and all above that sum in U. S. demand notes, redeemable in coin. It is needless to add, that we never saw any more hard money during the war. While the money lasted, the sutler did a flourishing business on the cash basis, but it was not of long duration; for he was soon compelled to adopt the credit system again.

The fall we went to Camp Dennison was warm and dry, until late in the season, when it turned cold and very wet. This, with the heavy guard-duty to perform, produced considerable sickness. The latter part of January, from twenty-five to thirty men were on the sick list in each company, and the quarters had the appearance of a hospital. The general health did not improve much until the middle of February, although none of the cases proved fatal at the time. The close confinement to camp, and the strict discipline, made the Regiment very restless, and in the latter part of January recruiting had almost come to a stand-still. The companies that had their complement of men were: companies A, Capt. Parker, Highland county; B, Capt. Warner, Delaware county; C, Capt. Frazee, Highland county; D, Capt. Elwood,

Clinton county ; E, Capt. Ireland, Miami county ; F, Capt. Moats, Defiance county ; G, Capt. Miller, Brown county ; K, Capt. Peterson, Cincinnati ; leaving H and I scarcely organized. But a call had been made for troops for the South-west, therefore the two companies were made up by transferring the surplus from those companies that had over eighty-two men.

The companies were lettered and occupied their positions in the Regiment in the rotation of the alphabet, and remained so during the service. It has been stated that but one other regiment from Ohio had been organized in the same manner.

The Regiment having its full number of companies, and the required number of men to entitle it to the full complement of field and staff officers, Governor Dennison made the following appointments: Peter J. Sullivan, Colonel ; J. R. Parker, Lieut.-Col. ; Jas. S. Wise, Major ; M. F. Cary, Surgeon ; A. A. Johnson, Ass't Surgeon ; R. C. McGill, Adjutant ; W. E. Brayman, Quartermaster ; John F. Spence, Chaplain. Col. Sullivan appointed the following non-commissioned staff: H. C. Stewart, Quartermaster Serg't.; Ed. Conklin, Serg't. Major; Doctor Boone, Hospital Steward. At considerable expense, silver cornet instruments were purchased for the Band, which had been recruited for the Regiment.

Camp life was getting to be very monotonous and irksome, and the time seemed long to us, lying thus inactive in camp, while every train was loaded with troops going to the front, to engage in active service. Our ideas of war, then, were rather of a romantic order. A skirmish, we supposed, would be a recreation, and a battle a real enjoyment, and some were even worried for fear the war would be over before we arrived, and peace declared before we ever fired a gun. But these romantic notions passed away, in the active service which soon followed.

CHAPTER III.

Marching Orders — Steamboat Ride Down the Ohio — Paducah — Without Arms — Rumors of an Attack — Armed with Austrian Rifles — Up the Tennessee — Fort Henry — Hog Mountain — First Shot — Savannah — Pittsburg Landing — Death of Capt. Ireland — Rebel Graves — Disembarking — First Camp.

SUNDAY, February 16, 1862, while at Divine service in Company K's quarters, we received orders to leave the following morning, for Paducah, Ky. All was now bustle and confusion. There were letters to write, rations to cook, knapsacks to pack, teams to load, &c., &c., but at it we went with enthusiasm, and by hard work we were ready at the appointed time. What it took us then twenty-four hours to do, we accomplished afterward at a moment's warning. We did not get started until 2:15 P. M., leaving the sick behind in the hospital. We arrived in Cincinnati at 3 P. M., marched through the lower part of the city, and halted at the public landing. Companies B, C, D and E, embarked on the steamer Hastings, the rest of the Regiment and the Band on the steamer Argonaut.

The boats being small, we were necessarily very much crowded. Left Cincinnati during the night, and owing to the novelty of the trip, we were all out at early dawn, on the hurricane deck, to get a glimpse of the country. The sun rose beautifully, but the air was cold. After roll-call on the hurricane deck, we spread our blankets and lay down in the sun to enjoy our free ride. We passed Louisville in the evening, and on account of the low stage of the river, we had some difficulty in getting over the falls. The following day it commenced raining and turned to sleet in the afternoon, which made it very unpleasant outside of the cabin.

We arrived at Paducah, Ky., the following day, Feb. 20th, disembarked, and marched up the Tennessee river a half mile, and pitched our tents in the old camp of the 8th Mo. Reg't. We found it in good condition. The streets had been graveled, and rude furnaces were under each tent. We now commenced our picket, fatigue and guard duty in the enemy's country. We were still without arms, and when ordered on picket were compelled to use old, worthless muskets. There was not even a sufficient supply of that kind of arms, therefore we were compelled to transfer them to each succeeding relief.

Sending us into the enemy's country without arms created considerable dissatisfaction in the Regiment. Rumors came in thick, that the Rebels, who were in strong force at Columbus, Ky., only thirty miles distant, were preparing for an attack on Paducah. We remained in camp, engaged in drilling, fatigue, guard and picket duty, until March 5th, when we were armed with the Austrian

Rifle, which proved to be an inferior gun, especially for continued, rapid firing. We were drilled in the manual of arms, and all preparations were made to repel an attack from the enemy.

March 6th, we were ordered up the Tennessee River. We were placed in the 4th Brigade, 5th Division, Army of the Tennessee. The Brigade was composed of the 48th, 70th and 72d Reg'ts. O. V. I., and commanded by Col. R. P. Buckland, of the 72d, Gen. W. T. Sherman commanding the Division. In organizing the Division and Brigade, Lieuts. Partridge and Coverdale were detached on staff duty, which severed their connection with the Regiment.

We embarked on the steamer Empress, which had a supply of commissary stores, also 200 head of beef cattle for the army. The sick were left behind in the Gothic Hospital. We proceeded up the Tennessee river to Fort Henry, where the army was concentrating, and arrived there the following day, March 8th. The steamer moved about six miles up the river, where the Regiment was permitted to disembark, to enable the soldiers to cook their rations, and practice with the new Austrian rifles. Some of the Regiment did not stop at target-practice, but tried their skill on a lot of hogs. This was the first foraging that the Regiment indulged in. In referring to that place afterward, it was designated as "Hog Mountain." In the eveing the boat dropped back to Fort Henry.

On the 9th the fleet, consisting of eighty-two

steamers, loaded with troops, started up the river, passing the Memphis and Ohio Railroad bridge, which had been burned to the water's edge a short time previous. We arrived at Savannah, Tennessee, on the 11th, and were greeted by large crowds of citizens, who seemed to hail us with delight — especially the slaves.

The only incident worthy of note transpired on the 10th, as we were passing a high bank, where a number of women and children were cheering us, by waving their handkerchiefs. When just above them, among the cedars, there was heard the sharp crack of a musket and the whiz of the buck and ball. One buck-shot was extracted from the coat-collar of one of the Regiment, who was standing near the bow of the boat. The rebel made good his escape, through the timber. This being the first shot the regiment had received from the Rebels, it created considerable excitement.

On the 13th, our Division was ordered up to Eastport, Miss., to cut the Memphis and Charleston R. R. and thus prevent Gen. A. S. Johnston from reinforcing the rebel forces, under command of Gen. Beauregard, who were encamped at Corinth, Miss., which is the junction of the Mobile & Ohio and the Memphis & Charleston R. R. The plan was abandoned, on account of the heavy rains and high waters, and we returned to Pittsburg Landing on the 15th of March. Capt. Ireland, who had been sick for several days, died that night, and was buried with military honors the following day, Sabbath. This was the first death in the Regiment, that had occurred in the South.

During the day we visited the battle-ground of the gun-boat engagement, that took place on the first of the month, and saw the graves of the rebel dead. Their burial had been hurried, for they were but a few inches under ground, and many of their faces were exposed to view.

Tuesday morning, March 18th, after a confinement of twelve days on board the boat, we disembarked at Pittsburg Landing. The only buildings there were a store-house, a grocery and a dwelling. From here roads led to the neighboring villages of Corinth and Purdy. The rebels had erected a battery on the high bluffs above the landing some months previous, but it had been captured by the gun-boats on the first of March. We camped a half mile from the river, where we remained three days.

CHAPTER IV.

BATTLE OF SHILOH.

Camp at Shiloh Church — Reconnoisance — Lieut. Greer Captured — Orders for Strict Watch — Battle Imminent — The Attack of April 6th — Long-Roll — In Line of Battle — To the Support of the Pickets — Counter-March — Second Line of Battle — The Rebel Charge and Repulse — Arrival of Capt. Hammond — Orders to Retreat — New Position — Repulse of the Enemy — Camp of the 81st Ohio — Arrival at the Landing — Advance to Support a Battery — Arrival of Gen. Buell's Troops — The Rebel Charge — Their Repulse and Retreat — Night — Rain.

THE day before we disembarked, Gen. Grant relieved Gen. C. F. Smith, who had been placed in command of the expedition when we left Paducah. He was relieved on account of sickness, of which he died soon after.

On the 21st we advanced about four miles to a new camp, situated in a light-timbered woods, about one hundred rods to the right of the Shiloh church, which stood on the brow of a hill, sloping southward. At its base, and nearly two hundred yards in our front, was Owl Creek. To the left, and in front of the church, the third brigade of our Division was camped; on our left the 70th Ohio, and to the right the 72d Ohio.

The whole country, from the Landing to the fortifications around Corinth, was a dense forest, except where a few small plantations had been cleared. Our first duty, after pitching tents, was picket; then followed brigade review by Gen. Sherman; also, company and battalion drill, and fatigue duty, until Thursday, April 3d, when our Brigade made a reconnoisance about five miles on the road to Corinth. We halted near a point where the road forked, and formed in line of battle. Two companies from the Regiment advanced as skirmishers, and were soon engaged with the rebel cavalry; but as the orders were *"not to be drawn into battle,"* the skirmishers fell back to the Brigade, and we returned to camp, arriving a little before dark. The next day, April 4th, at about 2 P. M., the left of our picket-line was attacked by the enemy's cavalry, and eight of the 70th Ohio were captured, together with Lieut. Greer, of the 48th, who was on Col. Buckland's staff.

The long-roll beat, and we were hurried on double-quick to the picket-line. Arriving there, we formed in line of battle with the Brigade, and waited for the attack. But the rebels, after having made a dash on our pickets, retreated in haste, losing several killed and wounded, and a few prisoners.

Saturday, the 5th, all was quiet during the day, until about 5 o'clock P. M., when the long-roll beat again. We immediately formed on our color-line, and remained an hour, when the firing ceased, and we were dismissed, with orders to fall in line at a moment's warning.

These frequent attacks on the pickets, and the bold manner in which the rebel cavalry maneuvered in our front, convinced us that their army was in force in our immediate front. The pickets were strengthened, and the officers of the camp-guard received strict orders to notify Col. Sullivan of any picket-firing during the night; and it is needless to add, that every one in the Regiment felt that we were on the eve of a battle. But during the night all was unusually still. No long-roll or bugle-sound disturbed the slumbering camp.

At early dawn on the morning of the 6th, Company C was notified at roll-call, to prepare for picket duty that day. While at breakfast, between 6 and 7 o'clock, the occasional picket-firing on our left, which had been kept up since daylight, increased to volleys. The long-roll beat, and with our usual promptness the Regiment formed on the color-line. During this time the rattle of musketry and roar of artillery became almost deafening on our left. In about twenty minutes the pickets in our front commenced firing, which told us the enemy was advancing, when Col. Buckland ordered our Regiment forward to their support. The head of the Regiment had scarcely reached Owl Creek, when we discovered the enemy, by their glistening bayonets, forming in line of battle on our side of the creek. We countermarched and formed on the left of the 72d Ohio, who were then about a hundred yards in front of their color-line, and in line of battle, facing the enemy. The left of our Regiment was scarcely in line, when the rebels, who were not more than a hundred yards distant, opened on our ranks, killing and wounding a number of the Regiment at their first fire.

Almost simultaneous with their first volley, came the discharge of our front rank, which was quickly followed by that of the rear. By this time the battle became general all along the line. We made use of what little shelter the trees and logs afforded, and continued to pour volley after volley into the rebel ranks, when they, receiving re-enforcements, attempted to charge on our lines, but were repulsed and driven back to the crest of the hill, where they took shelter again, returning our fire with that unabating fury that had been thinning our ranks since their first volley.

The Regiment, with the Brigade, held its ground against great odds, repulsing every charge until near 10 A. M., when the troops on our left were driven back, which exposed our left flank to an enfilading fire, that compelled us to fall back about a hundred yards to our color-line, where we fixed bayonets for a charge. While here, a battery of artillery came to our assistance, but soon left, without firing a gun. Just as the enemy began to press us on our left, Capt. Hammond, of Sherman's staff, rode up, complimented our Colonel and Regiment for their bravery, saying that ours was the first Regiment that he had found that had withstood the terrific fire, without being driven from their color-line. He said, Gen. Sherman's order was to fall back to the Purdy road, and then keep in line of the 72d Ohio, if it became necessary to retreat farther. We about-faced and retreated through our camp to the Purdy road..

We had scarcely halted, when a battery came dashing along the road at full speed, to our right. They had passed us but a short distance when they were captured. After falling back about half a mile, under a heavy fire, we took a stong position at the foot of a hill, in front of which was an open field, and from which we repulsed the enemy, causing them to fall back in disorder. We were now cut off from the river by the road. Behind us were the marshy bottoms of Owl Creek; in our front was the victorious rebel army; to our left, Pittsburg Landing. After a consultation, as we were detached from our Division, we took the nearest practicable route to the Landing.— During the retreat we were continually within musket and artillery range of the enemy. When we reached the camp of the 81st Ohio, the two wings of the Regiment that had been separated on the retreat, were reunited.

From here we were ordered to guard a bridge over Owl Creek, but had proceeded but a short distance when the order was countermanded, and we resumed our march to the Landing, where we arrived about an hour later. In the little strip of bottom below the Landing, we stacked our arms, and filled our canteens at the river, after which we fell in line and advanced to the front, and were greeted on all sides by deafening cheers by the troops, who thought we were the advance of Gen. Buell's army, who were then expected every moment. But when we told them we had been in the battle all day, their cheers died away, and they looked more gloomy than ever. Our army had been driven back all day, along our entire line, until about 4 o'clock P. M., when all our artillery was formed in a semi-circle of about a mile in length, with half that distance from the center to the Landing.

We had marched to the front to support a battery of siege guns, but no sooner had we occupied our position, than the enemy opened on us a frightful fire from their artillery. They then entered the ravine in our front, to make the final charge, and drive us into the Tennessee river. Then came the "rebel yell," that we had heard so often that day, and we knew that the charge would follow. After that there was a perfect calm. We could hear the heavy tramp of the rebel columns advancing on double-quick. The next moment our cannoneers sprang to their posts and discharged their double-shotted guns, loaded with grape and canister, at the rebel ranks, not more than fifty yards distant, while the infantry poured forth an incessant fire of musketry. The ground seemed to tremble, and the woods before us were swept by a storm of shell and canister. Men and horses succumbed to the withering fire, and when the smoke cleared away the rebels were seen in full retreat, flying in every direction.

During this charge the troops under Gen. Buell began to arrive. They dropped their knapsacks and gave the enemy a parting volley. But the day of carnage had now closed, and darkness and rain came down on the dead and dying, who lay on the battle-field of Shiloh. Thus ended one of the bloodiest days of the war.

After receiving a few crackers, the Regiment was ordered forward. Groping our way through the darkness for about a mile, we lay down in line of battle, ready to renew the conflict on the coming morrow. But little sleep did we get, between the rain and the continued cannonading of the gun-boats, mingled with the groans of the wounded and dying.

The rebels occupied our camps that night, for Gen. Beauregard, in his official report of the battle, says:

"I accordingly established my headquarters at the Church at Shiloh, in the enemy's encampment, with Gen. Bragg, and directed our troops to sleep on their arms, in such positions, in advance and rear, as corps commanders should determine, hoping from news received by special dispatch, that delays had been encountered by Gen. Buell in his march from Columbia, and that his main forces therefore could not reach the field of battle in time to save Gen. Grant's shattered fugitive forces from capture or destruction the following day. About six o'clock on the morning of the 7th of April, however, a hot fire of musketry and artillery opened from the enemy's quarter on our advance line, assured me of the junction of his forces, and soon the battle raged with such fury as satisfied me I was attacked by a largely superior force."

CHAPTER V.

THE BATTLE CONTINUED.

Battle of the Seventh — The Final Rout — Reoccupying Our Camps — The Battle-field — Burial of the Dead — Following the Enemy on the Eighth — The Attack on the 77th Ohio — The 48th Ohio to Their Support — Return to Camp — Our Dead and Wounded — Extracts from the Cincinnati Dailies — The Battle No Surprise — Loss in Both Armies — Extracts from Gen. Sherman's Official Report — Arrival of the Sanitary Commission — Gen. Halleck Takes Command — Band Discharged — Drill.

DURING the night the army was reinforced by the arrival of the remainder of the troops under Generals Buell and Wallace.

At early dawn on the following morning, we advanced with our Division, and met the enemy at 9 A. M. Their artillery was posted on a ridge, commanding an open field, which their batteries could rake from end to end. We charged over on double-quick, under a heavy artillery fire, and took possession of a piece of timber on the opposite side. Our batteries were soon brought to the front, when a regular artillery duel followed, which lasted about two hours, and at times became almost deafening, sending the shell and solid shot crashing through the timber, and tearing up the ground around us. Our troops being placed in supporting distance, were in better positions to assist each other than on the previous day, and at each attack of the rebels they were met by an equal force, and thus gradually they were compelled to yield the ground they had driven us from the day before. It was near 1 o'clock P. M. when they began cautiously to retreat, making a stand at every advantageous point, and delivering their fire with considerable effect, but being hotly pressed by our army, they finally gave way at about 4 P. M., and the rout became general. Our cavalry started in pursuit, following the retreating enemy several miles toward Corinth.

The enemy was already in retreat, and victory nearly won, when Col. Sullivan had his left arm shattered by a musket-ball, and Capt. Warner, of Company B, a brave and daring officer, was killed.

We then proceeded to take possession of our old camp, which we found in utter confusion, owing to the two days' battle over the same ground, and the occupation of our tents Sunday night by the enemy. In our absence our private property, including clothing, had been carried away. Our camp and the battle-field was a heart-sickening sight. The bodies of dead horses and wrecks of wagons, caissons, guns, and all kinds of war implements, were strewn over the battle-field. The dead were lying in every conceivable shape.— Some had fallen with their guns fast in their hands; others had received the messenger of death, and with their life-blood ebbing away, had sought the shelter of logs and trees, and laid down to die.

At one place, five rebels had found shelter behind a small tree, one behind the other in a row, when a cannon-ball struck a root in front of them, and glancing upward, passed diagonally through each one—the first at the hips, and the last at the head, severing it from the body ! But why dwell longer on the horrid sights that met the gaze all around?

That night, hungry and weary, we slept once more in our old camp. Early next morning, the 8th, we buried the dead in front of the position we held on Sunday morning. Twenty graves were dug, where we buried the dead of our Regiment, and seventy dead rebels were buried in one long trench.

At 8 o'clock A. M. the Regiment was ordered forward with the Division, to follow up the retreating enemy, in the direction of Corinth. After marching about a mile, we came to the camp that the rebels occupied on Saturday night. All along our line of march, could be seen remains of the retreating rebels, fresh-made graves, and the wounded and unburied dead. We had marched about five miles, when the 77th Ohio, who were in advance, were suddenly attacked in an open cotton-field, by the rebel cavalry, and overpowered by superior numbers. We were ordered on double-quick to their support. When we emerged from the woods the rebels retreated in haste, leaving the field to our possession. The 77th lost, in killed, wounded and prisoners, one-third their number, and, but for our prompt arrival, the whole Regiment would have been annihilated. Among the captured was Capt. McCormick, who was afterward a prisoner at Camp Ford, Texas. We halted on the opposite side of the field, and remained in line of battle until near dark. This engagement went by the name of "Fallen Timber," from the many trees that lay over the field. We returned to our camp that evening, reaching it about 11 o'clock.

The entire route was through mud and mire, and covered with guns, ammunition, disabled artillery, baggage wagons, &c. &c. We recaptured a number of the sick and wounded of the Regiment, who had been captured on the 6th. This ended the fighting at Shiloh.

Jesse Nelson, our drummer-boy, who was but a stripling youth, when the battle began threw down his drum and stepped into the ranks, with a rifle. He was shot through the head by a musket-ball, early in the engagement, while on his knees, in the act of firing.

The first verse of the poem, published shortly after the battle, entitled "The Drummer-Boy of Shiloh," is very appropriate:

> "On Shiloh's dark and bloody ground
> The dead and wounded lay;
> Among them was a drummer-boy,
> Who beat the drum that day."

The Regiment lost twenty killed, ninety wounded, and two taken prisoners. The following is a list of the casualties among the officers:

Killed: Capt. Warner, of Co. B. Mortally wounded: Capt. Bond, Co. I. Wounded: Col. Sullivan, Lieut. Posegate, Co. A, Lieuts. Lindsey and Plyley, Co. B; and Surgeon Carey, taken prisoner, while taking care of the wounded.

The following extracts are taken from the Cincinnati Times and Gazette, giving an account of the part taken by the 48th Ohio in the Battle of Shiloh:

Cincinnati Daily Times, April 10, 1862.

" PITTSBURG LANDING, April 7, 1862.

* * * * "In regard to those troops raised in our vicinity, I must say that all acquitted themselves most valiantly. The 48th, under Col. Sullivan, was among the very first whose camp was invaded, and even after the Regiments on either side had fallen back, they retired in good order, fighting every step of the way, to the line of the Second Division. It should be remembered that this is the first time they were ever brought into battle, and from the suddenness of the attack your readers may judge that the introduction was not one calculated to steady the nerves of raw troops. At one time during the contest, it was rumored that every officer of the 48th was killed; but they turned up in time to gather their men to the number of 250, and after a bivouac upon the wet ground last night, they led them again to the field to-day.

Col. Sullivan returns to-night with a wound in his left arm, but not at all dangerous, although quite painful. He will be all right again in a few days. Gen. Sherman yesterday complimented the Colonel, also Lieut Col. Parker, of Highland county, Maj. Wise, Adjutant Robt. McGill, and the men, as a body, by saying that even older Regiments could not have conducted themselves more nobly.
* * * E. M. S."

Highland News, April 24, 1862, copied from the Cincinnati Gazette.

"It was on Monday, during that terrible contest, that Col. Sullivan, while bravely rallying his Regiment, was wounded and borne from the field, and the brave and much-lamented Capt. Warner, of Co. B, fell with a Minie ball through the head. A better officer and more noble-hearted man, we had not in the Regiment. Lieut. Col. Parker won the entire esteem and confidence of the Regiment, as a man of cool and daring bravery. At all times during the conflict he was ever ready to cheer and rally by his presence, and his sword ever found in the thickest of the fight. In a word, the entire Regiment deserves the highest meed of praise.— To this Gen. Sherman has already subscribed by saying, the 48th and 72d Ohio maintained their ground longer than any other Regiment in his division.

"The Band boys, like true patriots, threw down their instruments, took up guns and went into the fight. Two of their number, Wm. Purdy and E. Henry, were mortally wounded, and died from the effects of their wounds a short time after."

THE BATTLE NO SURPRISE.

We had penetrated about 225 miles up the Tennessee river, in the enemy's country. Corinth, our objective point, was but thirty miles distant, strongly fortified and garrisoned, by an army estimated between fifty and sixty thousand men, under Gen. Beauregard. We have already shown that on April 3d our brigade was sent out to reconnoiter. We found the enemy in strong force, within about five miles of our camp, but we were instructed not to bring on an engagement. April 4th, our picket-line was attacked by the rebel cavalry, which resulted in a loss of a few killed, wounded and prisoners, on each side. Saturday, the 5th, on account of the heavy picket-firing another alarm was sounded, at about 5 P. M., which was caused by the near approach of the rebel cavlary.

That night, Col. Sullivan instructed the Sergeant of the camp-guard to notify him, at once, if an alarm was given during the night. The following morning, Sunday, April 6th, the reveille was sounded as usual at daylight, and roll-call followed.— While at breakfast the long-roll beat, and we immediately formed on our color line. While in line, those who had not finished their breakfast, returned to their tents and finished their meals. We had been in line half an hour, when we were ordered to the front, to support the pickets, and had proceeded but a short distance, when we saw the enemy advancing in force. We returned to our brigade, reformed our line, and the battle commenced.

Our forces, the first day, numbered 32,000, and and the enemy 45,000 men. Both sides received reinforcements for the second day's battle. The rebels were armed, principally, with U. S. muskets, and their ammunition consisted of one ball and three buck-shot.

Previous to the battle, Gen. Beauregard had issued an order to his troops, a copy of which was found in one of our tents, the first section of which reads as follows :

" Field and company officers are specially enjoined to instruct their men to fire *at the feet of the enemy!* They will thus avoid over-shooting, and besides, wounded men give more trouble to our adversary than his dead, as they have to be taken from the field."

The loss in our Division was 318 killed, 1275 wounded and 440 missing. Our entire loss in killed and wounded, according to official reports, was 10,600 ; and Beauregard places his at 10,699 ; besides the prisoners taken on both sides, our loss in prisoners being the greatest. The total loss of both armies is estimated at 25,000 men, which was a frightful loss in proportion to the number engaged. This battle exploded the Southern assertion that one Southerner was a match for five Northern soldiers, and also taught the Western army, that all the advantages gained over their adversary would have to be won by desperate, hard fighting.

The following is an extract from the official report of Gen. Sherman, of the Battle of Shiloh :

[From Gen. Sherman's Memoirs.]

"HEADQUARTERS FIFTH DIVISION, }
CAMP SHILOH, April 10th, 1862. }

" *Capt. J. A. Rawlins, Ass't. Adj't. Gen. to Gen. Grant:*

" SIR— * * * On Sunday morning early, the 6th inst., the enemy drove our advance-guard back on the main body, when I ordered under arms all my Division.

" Shortly after 7 A. M., with my entire staff, I rode along a portion of our front, and when in the open field, before Appler's regiment, the enemy's pickets opened a brisk fire upon my party, killing my orderly. * * *

"About 8 A. M. I saw the glistening bayonets of heavy masses of infantry to our left front, in the woods beyond the small stream alluded to, and became satisfied for the first time that the enemy designed a determined attack on our whole camp.— All of the regiments of my Division were then in line of battle at their proper posts. * * *

" The battle opened by the enemy's battery, in the woods to our front, throwing shells into our camp. Taylor's and Waterhouse's batteries promptly responded, and I then observed heavy battalions of infantry passing obliquely to the left, across the open field in Appler's front; also other columns directly upon my Division. Our infantry and artillery opened along the whole line, and the battle became general. * * *

"Although our left was thus turned, and the enemy was pressing our whole line, I deemed Shiloh so important that I remained by it, and renewed my orders to Colonels McDowell and Buckland to hold their ground, and we did hold these positions until about 10 A. M., when the enemy had got his artillery to the rear of our left flank and some change became necessary. Two regiments of Hildebrand's brigade — Appler's and Mungen's — had already disappeared to the rear, and Hildebrand's own regiment was in disorder. I therefore gave orders for Taylor's battery, still at Shiloh, to fall back as far as the Purdy and Hamburg road, and for McDowell and Buckland to adopt that road as their new line. I rode across the angle and met Behr's battery at the cross-road, and ordered it immediately to come into battery action right.— Capt. Behr gave the order, but was almost immediately shot from his horse, when drivers and gunners fled in disorder, carrying off the caissons, and abandoning five out of six guns, without firing a shot. The enemy pressed on, gaining this battery, and we were again forced to choose a new line of defense. Hildebrand's brigade had substantially disappeared from the field, though he himself bravely remained. McDowell's and Buckland's brigade maintained their organization, and were conducted by my aids, so as to join on Gen. McClernand's right, thus abandoning my original camps and line. This was about 10½ A. M., at which time the enemy had made a furious attack on Gen. McClernand's whole front. He struggled most determinedly, but finding him pressed, I moved McDowell's brigade against the left flank of the enemy, forced him back some distance, and then directed the men to avail themselves of every cover, trees, fallen timber, and a wooded valley to our right. We held this position for four long hours, sometimes gaining and at other times losing ground, Gen. McClernand and myself acting in perfect concert, and struggling to maintain this line.

"While we were so hard pressed, two Iowa regiments approached our rear, but could not be brought up to the severe fire that was raging in our front, and Gen. Grant, who visited us on that ground, will remember our situation about 3 P. M.; but about 4 P. M. it was evident that Hurlburt's line had been driven back to the river, and knowing that Gen. Lew Wallace was coming with reinforcements from Crump's Landing, Gen. McClernand and I, on consultation, selected a new line of defense, with its right covering a bridge by which Gen. Wallace had to approach. We fell back as well as we could, gathering in addition to our own such scattered forces as we could find, and formed a new line. * * * I had a clear field, about two hundred yards wide, in my immediate front, and contented myself with keeping the enemy's in-

fantry at that distance during the rest of the day.
" In this position we rested for the night. My
command had become decidedly of a mixed character. Buckland's brigade was the only one that
retained its organization. Col. Hildebrand was
personally there, but his brigade was not. Col.
McDowell had been severely injured by a fall
from his horse, and had gone to the river, and the
three regiments of his brigade were not in line.
* * * Generals Grant and Buell visited me in
our bivouac that evening, and from them I learned
the situation of officers on other parts of the field.
Gen. Wallace arrived from Crump's Landing shortly after dark, and formed his line to my right rear.
It rained hard during the night, but our men were
in good spirits, lay on their arms, being satisfied
with such bread and meat as could be gathered
at the neighboring camps, and determined to redeem on Monday the losses on Sunday. * * *

"At daylight on Monday I received General
Grant's order to advance and recapture our original camps. I dispatched several members of my
staff to bring up all the men they could find, and
reoccupied the ground to the extreme right of
Gen. McClernand's, where we attracted the fire of
a battery located near Col. McDowell's former
headquarters. Here I remained, patiently waiting
for the sound of Gen. Buell's advance upon the
main Corinth road. About 10 A. M. the heavy
firing in that direction and its steady approach
satisfied me, and Gen. Wallace being on our right

flank, with his well-conducted Division, I led the head of my column to Gen. McClernand's right, formed line of battle, facing south, with Buckland's brigade directly across the ridge, and Stuart's brigade on its right in the woods, and thus advanced, steadily and slowly, under a heavy fire of musketry and artillery. Taylor had just got to me from the rear, where he had gone for ammunition, and brought up three guns, which I ordered into position, to advance by hand-firing. Under cover of their fire, we advanced till we reached the point where the Corinth road crosses the line of McClernand's camp, and here I saw for the first time the well-ordered and compact columns of Gen. Buell's Kentucky forces, whose soldierly movements at once gave confidence to our newer and less disciplined men.

"This was about 2 P. M. The enemy had one battery close by Shiloh, and another near the Hamburg road, both pouring grape and canister upon any column of troops that advanced upon the green point of water-oaks. Willich's regiment had been repulsed, but a whole brigade of McCook's Division advanced, beautifully deployed, and entered this dreaded wood. I ordered my second brigade to form on its right, and my fourth brigade, Col. Buckland,* on its right, all to advance abreast with this Kentucky brigade, before mentioned, which I afterward found to be Rousseau's brigade of McCook's Division. I gave per-

*To which the 48th Ohio was attached.

sonal direction to the twenty-four pounder guns, whose well-directed fire first silenced the enemy's guns to the left, and afterward at the Shiloh meeting-house. Rousseau's brigade moved in splendid order steadily to the front, sweeping everything before it, and at 4 P. M. we stood upon the ground of our original front line, and the enemy was in full retreat. I directed my several brigades to resume at once their original camps. * * *

"My Division was made up of regiments perfectly new, nearly all having received their muskets for the first time at Paducah. None of them had ever been under fire, or beheld heavy columns of an enemy bearing down on them, as they did on last Sunday.

* * * "Col. Buckland managed his brigade well. I commend him to your notice as a cool, intelligent and judicious gentleman, needing only confidence and experience to make a good commander. His subordinates, Colonels Sullivan (48th Ohio) and Cockerill, (70th Ohio), behaved with great gallantry; the former receiving a wound on Sunday, and yet commanding and holding his regiment well in hand all day on Monday, until his right arm was broken by a shot. Col. Cockerill held a larger proportion of his men than any Colonel in my division, and was with me from first to last. * * *

"I am, with much respect, your obedient servant, W. T. SHERMAN,
"Brig. Gen. Com'dg Fifth Division."

A week after the battle the Sanitary Commission began to arrive, with supplies for the sick and wounded. With them came Dr. S. J. Spees, of Lynchburg, Ohio. Our Surgeon, Dr. Cary, had been taken prisoner, leaving all the care of the sick and wounded on Assistant Surgeon, A. A. Johnson. The sick list increased very rapidly, caused by the fatigue and exposure of the three days' battle, together with the heavy rains and damp weather. Over one-half of the Regiment was unable for duty.

In the mean time, Gen. Halleck had arrived at Pittsburg Landing, and assumed command of the combined armies of Grant and Buell, leaving Gen. Grant second in command. He issued a general order for every regiment to attend battalion drill in the morning, and brigade and division drill in the afternoon. From these drills none were excused, unless unable to sit up. Those unable to march were hauled out to the drill-ground in ambulances, where they could watch the maneuvers.

On the 15th of April, a general order was issued to discharge all regimental bands, excepting one to each brigade. When the battle of Shiloh commenced, our band discarded their fine instruments, armed themselves, and went into the fight with the Regiment. The result was, they lost their instruments, and had two of their number killed. Having no instruments, they were one of the first bands discharged, much to the regret of the whole Regiment.

April 16th, all the sick and wounded of the Regiment were sent North. The army was now thoroughly drilled in division, brigade and battalion drill, as well as picket-duty and the art of constructing field defenses, which was a great advantage to us in the advance on Corinth, as Gen. Halleck had decided to approach by regular siege, that was necessarily slow and attended with a great deal of labor. The 48th Ohio bore its full share of duty in picketing, constructing earthworks, and reconnoitering.

CHAPTER VI.

On the Road to Corinth — Order to March — Joke on Sergeant Reed — First Earthworks — Second Advance — Camp Number Six — Engagement at the Russell House — Talk with the Rebel Pickets — Separation of Mother and Child — Last Line of Earthworks — Evacuation of Corinth — The Pursuit and Return — Comparison of the Two Armies.

APRIL 29th, we received marching orders, and moved with the Division towards Corinth, Miss., leaving a very large number of the Regiment sick in the tents, who were sent home a few days later by the Sanitary Commission.

We marched about six miles and camped.— May 1st, the following order was issued to the Army: " The troops will at once be prepared for a rapid march, and each soldier will carry three days' rations in his haversack, and the wagons four days' rations additional. The baggage will be limited to two tents for each company for all purposes, the allowance of axes and spades, and such cooking utensils as are absolutely necessary. The soldiers will carry their blankets only, leaving their knapsacks in camp. One hundred and forty rounds of ammunition will be taken along—forty rounds in the cartridge boxes, and one hundred rounds in the wagons ; and on the eve of a battle forty additional rounds will be issued each man, to be carried on his person."

During our stay here an amusing incident occurred. Serg't. Reed, of Co. B, received information from some wag in the Regiment that he had been promoted to Second Lieutenant. He immediately procured his shoulder-straps, and proposed to treat the Company in honor of the event, but on going to the sutler, he found that he had sold everything except some stale butter. In the absence of something better, he purchased fifteen or twenty pounds and distributed it to his Company. After he had aired his straps, to the delight of the Regiment, for several days, the joke leaked out, and none laughed more than he when he discovered the sell.

May 3d, we received two months' pay, being the second payment in the service. On the 4th, we received four days' rations. The crackers proved to be mouldy and worm-eaten. On the 5th we were ordered to advance, which we did with great caution, and camped toward evening. In the mean time a heavy rain set in and continued, without intermission, for fifteen hours. After we we had selected our camp and made shelters to protect us from the rain, orders were received to send a strong force of the Regiment on picket, which was not agreeable news in the face of a driving rain. Through some misunderstanding we were taken to the wrong picket-line, and were afterward transferred to the reserve, in an open field, near a fence, which we used in making shelter. On returning to camp the following day, we learned that the high waters had swept away the bridges between us and the Landing; also, that the four days' damaged rations, issued on the 4th, would have to last us eight days. We cut the timber in our front, and constructed earthworks, but had scarcely completed them when we advanced one mile on the following day, and built a new line of defenses. Our arms were always stacked convenient while we were at work. Every morning at four o'clock we were in our fortifications, prepared for an attack, and remained there for two hours.

Capt. Frazee, having recovered from his sickness, returned for duty and took command of the Regiment. May 12th we occupied Camp Number Five, seven miles from Corinth. We spent every night in our rifle-pits, prepared for a night attack. The alarms and long-rolls were frequent, but did not lead to any general engagement. May 13th we advanced two miles and established a new line of defenses at Camp Number Six. May 17th we received orders to be ready for a reconnoisance in force with the 72d and 54th Ohio and 8th Missouri. We had proceeded but a short distance when the 54th Ohio, on our left, became hotly engaged.

The rebels were found in strong force at the Russell House. With the aid of artillery they were dislodged, and we drove them several miles.

At dark we fell back a short distance, and bivouacked for the night. We had taken no rations, but they were sent to us the next morning; and at noon we were back in camp again.

Our works here were very formidable. There were several batteries of heavy and light artillery in position. The 53d Ohio was added to our brigade, which was now commanded by Gen. J. W. Denver, and occupied the right of Gen. Sherman's Division.

May 20th, we made another advance, and established a new line a considerable distance to the right, designated as Camp Number Seven, where, with our usual promptness, we were soon in position behind our new works.

May 26th, while on picket near the Mobile & Ohio Railroad, we discovered the rebel pickets on the opposite side. Quite a number of us advanced to within speaking distance, keeping well protected behind the trees; we then opened fire on them, which they returned, with the remark that we were firing too high. It was kept up until toward evening, when we proposed to them to quit firing during the night, to which they consented. We kept a sharp look-out, but everything was quiet until daylight, when we heard a pack of hounds on the trail of a deer. It was coming at full speed toward our lines. As soon as it came in sight, D. Edginton fired, killing it instantly. That day we had venison for dinner. Soon after, a rebel picket inquired whether we had a daily paper. One of our men had a Cincinnati Commercial of May 20, '62. It was proposed that they could have the paper by coming after it. They met us on the railroad, leaving all arms and ammunition behind. Quite an interesting conversation passed between us; among other things, we agreed to have no more picket - firing in future — which agreement was sacredly kept on our end of the line. They stated that they had plenty to eat, and received whisky and coffee twice a week; that they were fighting for their rights and liberties; that the Union was "played out," and that Gen. Beauregard was in command, and Gen. Bragg second in command, at Corinth, which was four and one-half miles from our camp; that they were ready for us, and although the prospects looked gloomy, they were the boys to fight it out. They also asked the very impertinent question, whether we did not think that they were right and we wrong in regard to the war? The discussion was getting quite warm, when by mutual consent we changed the subject. After a half-hour's conversation we separated and returned to our picket lines. They were in plain view frequently during the day, but we did not molest them.

After the evacuation of Corinth, a citizen related to us that he was in Corinth and heard the rebel pickets telling of their adventure on the picket-line, the day after it took place. He said it was spoken of a great deal in the army, and the pickets were looked upon as the heroes of the day. In the evening we were relieved and returned to camp.

As we neared Corinth, the supply of water for the army became a problem. The water for man and beast was taken from the same stagnant pools in the almost dried-up small streams. The enemy, knowing our condition, fought desperately wherever a pond of any size was found.

During one of our advance movements, an interesting incident occurred. Lieut. Posegate, in command of Co. A, was sent forward as skirmishers. They had driven the rebels before them, and occupied a position between two farm-houses. A woman left her child in the house alone, while she went on an errand to a neighbor's house, situated between her home and our lines. During her brief absence our army had advanced, leaving her in our lines, and her dwelling and child half-way between the two contending armies, with every indication of a battle at hand. The woman was almost frantic for the safety of her child. She had been led to believe that the Yankees murdered all that came in their way. But through the kindness of Lieut. Posegate she reached her home in safety, and after thanking him for his services, she stated that no earthly consideration, except the thoughts of her child, would have induced her to pass between two armies facing each other, prepared for battle ; and if her husband, who was in the Southern Army at Corinth, knew how kindly she had been treated by the Union soldiers, he wouldn't remain in arms against us another day! No doubt the woman and child were removed to a place of safety, as they were never seen again.

On the 29th we moved forward with the army, driving the rebel out-posts before us for about a mile, and establishing a new line in a strip of timber on a slight elevation, from which their batteries attempted to dislodge us, but did not succeed. After the troops were all in position, our Regiment was ordered to support the 4th Indiana Battery, which kept up a heavy cannonading until dark, when their firing ceased and work on the earthworks commenced. The night being very dark, and no lights allowed, the line for the rifle pits was made by laying down rails six feet apart, and throwing out the ground between them. Our task was completed at midnight, when we lay upon our arms as usual, " to sleep, perchance to dream." A light breeze was blowing from the south, and during the night we could plainly hear the movement of trains on the Mobile & Ohio Railroad, bands playing, and see the rockets ascending in the air, signaling their out-posts, which clearly indicated that they were evacuating.

While at breakfast the following morning, May 30th, we heard heavy explosions in the direction of Corinth. The rebels were evidently destroying what could not be carried away. Soon the word came, " Corinth is evacuated."

The 48th and 72d Ohio received orders to advance immediately. After passing the pickets,

Companies A and B were sent forward as skirmishers, leaving Co. C at the right of the Regiment. After passing through a narrow strip of timber, we reached an open country, in which the fortifications of Corinth were located. When within fifty yards of their works we halted and gave three rousing cheers for the "old flag;" after which we advanced over the works on double-quick through dust and heat for about two miles, when we halted in sight of Corinth. As soon as the rest of our brigade arrived, we advanced again, the 48th and 72d taking the lead. We passed through Corinth, which we found smoldering in ruins, and halted a short distance beyond the town, near the forks of a road, where the rebels had gone to the trouble to put up a large fingerboard, with the inscription, "Take the road to the left." The enemy being out of our reach, and further pursuit by the infantry useless, we returned to our camp in the evening. The result of the capture of Corinth was the fall of Memphis and Fort Pillow. By getting in their rear it made both places untenable, and they fell an easy prey to the gunboat squadron.

The following description of the evacuation of Corinth is from a Southern history, "The War in the West:"

"Halleck dug and dug, and pulled his immense army forward slowly and painfully as a wounded snake. Steel met steel — gun answered gun in the pines around Hamburg, and the glitter of

bright bayonets, away over to the left, told a busy
story of Bragg's adventure and unceasing activity.
But an enemy invaded the heart of Beauregard's
camp, more terrible, more deadly, than Halleck's
vast host, if it had been doubled. It was the soldier's enemy — *disease.* The sultry sun, the putrid
water, the unwholesome food, the low, swampy
country, the unceasing duty, the long, eternal battle, *sapped* the *elan* of the young volunteers, and
filled the hospitals and the graveyards with the
best blood of the South.

"Train after train carried the miserable suffer-
ers southward, but train after train was still in demand, and the epidemic increased and the mortality was fearful. One hot, weary afternoon, Captain ——— received orders to call in all his out-
lying detachments, prepare three days rations, and
march directly on Corinth. A battle was deemed
inevitable, for latterly the skirmishes had been unusually severe, and ever and anon the hoarse voice
of the heavy Parrots could be heard, loud above
the noisy and more rapid discharges of the field
artillery. Corinth was reached at nightfall, and
the command slept on their arms just northward
of the town, the sentinels halting in their mechan-
ical beats long enough to catch the echoes of Halleck's distant signal-guns, and to watch the out-
post cavalry rockets going up among the clouds.

"Before daylight the next morning, a vast, compact column, sixteen deep, came from Bragg's
line on the left, and marched away in silence to-

ward Tupelo, followed by artillery, wagons, cavalry, and a sickly train of pale faces and emaciated bodies. It was Beauregard, evacuating Corinth before the pestilence, but not from fear of Halleck. The living tide surged past, all the long, hot day, and every step was proud, and every gun glistened brightly in the sun-light. A death-like silence pervaded the deserted streets; the usual cannonading on the left had ceased. Van Dorn's stubborn pickets no longer plied their vengeful rifles, and the patrolling cavalry hushed the clank of sabers and the shrill neighing of their lonesome steeds. The last regiment who left the *grave-girdled* town, marched in skirmish order, with their loaded guns and bayonets fixed."

This shows that Gen. Beauregard's army was in a fearful condition, and all the hardships and privations of the siege that they endured would apply to our own army in a still greater degree, for we were on the offensive and not acclimated, while they were on the defensive, fighting within sight of their own homes. But the condition of our army was never better during the siege.

Of the splendid condition of our army when we entered Corinth, Gen. Sherman says:—"I esteem it (the siege of Corinth) a magnificent drill, as it served for the instruction of our men in guard and picket duty, and in habituating them to out-door life, and by the time we had reached Corinth, I believe that army was the best then on this continent, and could have gone where it pleased."

CHAPTER VII.

On to Memphis — Visit of Thomas Peale, Esq. of Lynchburg — Return of Lieut. Col. Parker — La-Grange — Moscow — Lafayette — Newton and the Snake — Return to Moscow — March to Holly Springs and Return — Contrabands — On the March to Memphis — White Station — Memphis — Camp at Fort Pickering — Maj. Wise and Lieut. Fields Resign — Return of Absentees — On Provost Guard — Cincinnati Reported Captured — Trip to Randolph — Rebel Cotton Burners.

WE remained in camp until June 2d, when we took up our line of march to Memphis, leaving behind Capt. Frazee, who was sent home on sick-leave, which left Capt. Peterson in command of the Regiment. We were delayed a short time by a heavy shower. Passing through Corinth, we bivouacked on the road-side for the night.

Early the following morning, we were ordered to Chewalla on double-quick, a distance of eight or ten miles. Why we were ordered to that place on a run, with no enemy near, has never been satisfactorily explained.

On June 9th, Thomas Peale, Esq., of Lynchburg, Ohio, made us a visit, aud remained with us on the march to Lafayette, Tenn. From here he went with the supply train to Memphis, and from there home. He had quite an experience of army life.

June 9th, we resumed our march to Memphis, and camped at Tuscumbia river in the evening, where Lieut. Col. Parker, who had been sent home on sick-leave shortly after the battle of Shiloh, rejoined and took command of the Regiment. The following day, we repaired the bridge, which had been destroyed by the enemy. We left June 11th, marched through the richest portion of West Tennessee, and arrived at LaGrange June 14th. We left LaGrange on the 16th, and arrived at Moscow in the evening. Our chief employment, during our stay at Moscow, was to rebuild the railroad bridge over Wolf river.

On the 22d, we were ordered to Lafayette, eight miles below, on the Memphis & Charleston R. R., where we arrived in the afternoon. The following day a portion of the Regiment went on picket.— During the night quite an amusing incident occurred on one of the picket-posts. Thomas Newton was startled by a snake crawling up inside his pants. He raised the alarm and danced a lively jig, while his comrades assisted him to release the snake, but fortunately he sustained no other injury than a big scare, which he will never forget.

After we returned to camp the following morning, we learned that our brigade had been ordered back to Moscow. This proved to be the hottest and sultriest day of the season, and our march back *to* Moscow will be as long remembered by us as the one *from* Moscow, mentioned in history, will be remembered by the French. The blinding dust and intense heat were terribly severe on both man and beast. The roadside was lined with soldiers overcome by heat, and quite a number of artillery horses dropped dead in their traces.

Arriving at our destination, we camped on the banks of Wolf river. During our stay here we had a pleasant time, our duties being light and the bathing facilities excellent. On the 29th several took "French leave," taking the overland route for home, where they arrived safely, and in due season were safely returned to the Regiment again.

On the 30th of June, our Division was ordered on an expedition to Holly Springs, twenty-two miles south. We arrived in sight of Holly Springs at noon on the following day, while the cavalry was having a hot skirmish with the enemy. Our Regiment and the 4th Indiana Battery were ordered forward in the engagement, but a few well-directed shots from the artillery started the rebels in full retreat. We remained in our position until dark, when we fell back about three miles, and camped in the woods on the road-side. Here we lay in ambush, awaiting the return of the enemy, until July 5th, but they did not appear.

We started on the expedition with only one day's rations, and expected a supply from Memphis, by the supply-train, but the train had been attacked by the rebels and delayed. As foraging was almost unknown at this stage of the war, we were compelled to subsist entirely on blackberries and apples. We soon stripped the orchards in the vicinity, of their green fruit, and lived a few days on the refuse from a cavalry camp.

On the 6th we started back to Moscow. We marched until midnight, when we met the supply-train. A halt was ordered, and through the energy of H. C. Stewart, Quartermaster Sergeant, the rations were soon distributed to the hungry soldiers. At day-break on the following day, we were on the march, reaching Moscow at noon.

Up to this time, the slaves were still at work for their masters, and none were allowed to follow the army. On the Holly Springs expedition the Regiment engaged several of them as cooks, but they had scarcely been initiated when an order was issued to exclude all slaves from camp. Thus ended our first attempt at putting them to work to assist in putting down the Rebellion. But "De Year ob Jubilo," as the slaves called it, was fast approaching. In less than two months, there was a complete change. The slaves came into camp in droves, and were put to work as cooks, teamsters and laborers. At one time nearly every soldier in the Regiment had his private servant!

On the 18th of July, we took up our line of march once more for Memphis, camping at Collierville the first night, and at White's Station the second, where we remained the succeeding day— the Sabbath — and being short of rations, we spent nearly the whole time in cooking green corn. A field of twenty acres did not quite supply the demand for our Division.

The following day, July 21st, we resumed our march. Our Regiment guarded the wagon-train. When within a few miles of the city, we were ordered forward on double-quick, to rejoin our brigade, and make our entrance into the city with our Division. As it was an exceeding hot day, and the dust almost suffocating, it was with great difficulty that we succeeded in picking our way through the immense wagon-train that obstructed the entire road. On reaching our brigade, we entered the city of Memphis, with bands playing, colors flying, and the troops cheering. We marched to the south end of the city, and camped in a peach-orchard, in Fort Pickering, on the banks of the Mississippi river. It had been nearly six months since we had left Ohio, and in that time we had been constantly on the move, and had seen soldiering in nearly all its phases, and now we had reached a haven that promised us rest for a short season at least.

Memphis is a handsome city, built on a high bluff, 420 miles below St. Louis. It had a population of 20,000 before the war, and was the center of a vast trade. Gen. Jackson's equestrian statue is in a beautiful park, in the heart of the city, but the rebels had obliterated the inscription, " The Union must and shall be preserved." Shortly after arriving here, Dr. Boon, Hospital Steward, was discharged, and Jos. A. Gravatt appointed in his place.

August 1st, Col. Sullivan, with a large number of officers and soldiers, who had been home on sick-leave, returned for duty, which made the Regiment look like its former self again. On the 2d, the Paymaster arrived, and paid us two months pay. It came when it was most needed and was highly appreciated.

Sept. 2d, Adjutant McGill and Lieut. Posegate were sent to Ohio, with a recruiting party, consisting of one sergeant from each company. The day following, Major Wise resigned.

On the 4th, the Regiment was ordered on provost-guard duty in Memphis, companies C, H and G being stationed at the military prison in Irving Block. It contained one hundred rebel prisoners and a number of disorderly Union soldiers. Our duties were very severe, as we had to be on guard every alternate six hours, both day and night.

The Memphis Argus, of Sept. 7th, contained the following: "Cincinnati, Ohio, has surrendered to Gen. Kirby Smith." This was startling news to our Regiment. Out of the ten companies, one was raised in the city, and seven within a circle of sixty miles. Our only consolation was that it might turn out to be a false report, which fortunately proved to be true, as it was contradicted in the same paper a few days later.

Sept. 8th, Lieut. John Kean was discharged for disability. On the 11th, the rebel prisoners were sent to Vicksburg for exchange, and we returned to our camp in Fort Pickering. Before leaving, they were all furnished with new rebel uniforms by their friends.

Toward the latter part of the month, the duty of the Regiment became very laborious. Large details were made daily, to cut down all the timber within one mile of the fort, and to demolish all buildings within a half mile, in addition to regimental and brigade guards. On the 20th, the Regiment was sent twenty miles down the river, on a boat, to guard one hundred contrabands, while cutting and loading cane, which grew in abundance in the river bottoms, and was used by us in constructing fortifications.

When the weather got cooler, in October, our brigade and division drills occurred more frequently, including a " grand review " every Wednesday.

Oct. 17th, Lieut. Posegate and his recruiting party returned, with a number of new recruits for the Regiment. On the 18th, we enlarged our streets and prepared more comfortable quarters for the winter.

After the discharge of our cornet band at Shiloh, efforts were made to make our drum corps more efficient, but it was not successfully carried out until it was placed under the leadership of George McMahon, after arriving here. From that time forward, at intervals on a march and on entering towns and cities, the band struck up some patriotic air, which always elicited a hearty cheer from the Regiment.

Sept. 22d, Capt. Frazee took command of one hundred and fifty men of the Regiment, and went up the Mississippi river on a steamer to Randolph, to reinforce a regiment of cavalry that had left Memphis a week previous, on a raid. We disembarked and remained all night. During the evening the cavalry made their appearance. The next day we returned with the cavalry to Memphis.

On the 1st of November, the Regiment was ordered again on provost-guard. Companies B and C were stationed at the wharf, and guarded the Government stores. We occupied the Bradley Block, near the landing, for our quarters. During our stay the building took fire under the hearth, in the second story. The alarm was given, but before the engines arrived we had the fire under control. On the evening of the 4th, a strong guard was ordered out on patrol duty, in anticipation of a disturbance at the Warsham House. We patrolled the streets in that vicinity until midnight, but everything remained quiet; and after partaking of a free lunch at the hotel, and receiving tickets for breakfast, we returned to our quarters.

On the 7th, the Regiment was relieved and we returned to camp. Troops, under the President's last call, were now arriving, and by the 16th of November quite a large army was concentrated here, which was formed into divisions. Our Regment was placed in the 3d Brigade and 3d Division, under orders to be ready to march on the 26th of November, but on the 24th we were ordered on provost duty in the city, to relieve the 46th Ohio.

On the 26th, all the troops, except four or five regiments, left for Holly Springs, Miss. We remained in the city until the 29th, when we returned to camp. In the evening Companies A, B and C went on picket-duty, on the Pigeon Roost road, running south from Memphis, and remained two days.

The rebel cotton-burners, who had been at work, destroying all the cotton within the vicinity of Memphis, to keep it from falling into the hands of the Government, caught a drayman of the city, who had been engaged to go beyond the lines, to haul cotton from the neighboring plantations. The cotton was burned, and his mule and dray were confiscated. When he came through the picket-lines he informed us of his loss, when eight of the pickets volunteered to go with him and recapture his property. A barouche passing along was pressed into the service. About two miles out the property was found at an old plantation, and returned to the drayman, who, with many thanks, returned home, a happy man.

Dec. 5th, H. C. Stewart, Quartermaster Serg't., was discharged. He afterward served in the Q. M. Department until the close of the war.

CHAPTER VIII.

Expedition for Vicksburg — Marching Orders — Down the Mississippi — Milliken's Bend — Up the Yazoo — March Through the Swamps — First Attack on Vicksburg — Picketing — Evacuation — Up the Mississippi and Arkansas Rivers — Arkansas Post — Battle and Capture of the Garrison—Loss in Killed and Wounded.

ANOTHER expedition was now organized, under Gen. Sherman, for Vicksburg, to proceed by boats down the Mississippi river. As we were not yet assigned to any Division, we had concluded that we would spend Christmas at Memphis, and had written home to that effect. But on the 19th of December Lieut. Col. Parker made a request of Gen. Hurlbut, Commander of the Post, to have the Regiment relieved of garrison duty, so as to join the expedition. Such requests are always granted, and on the following day we were ordered on board the steamer "City of Alton." We were placed in the second brigade, with the 19th Ky., 77th, 97th, 108th and 130th Illinois regiments, commanded by Col. W. J. Landrum, of the 19th Ky., and in the Division commanded by Gen. A. J. Smith.

The Regiment was in command of Lieut. Col. Parker. Col. Sullivan, who was still suffering from his wound, had been appointed president of a military board, and was left behind. Lieut. Quartermail was also left, with several members of the Regiment, who were unable for duty.

On leaving Camp Dennison for active service, the Regiment had thirteen teams and five ambulances. But now we were only allowed five teams and one ambulance, which was shortly after still further reduced to two teams.

During Saturday the troops embarked on the boats. That night they were paid two months' pay, and on Sunday, Dec. 21st, 1862, the Division left at 2 P. M. Memphis, where we had spent the last five months, was soon lost to view. The boat ran until 1 o'clock that night, then tied up at Friar's Point, twelve miles below Helena, Ark. Here the fleet of forty-five transports, loaded with troops, and several gun-boats, joined us. The whole fleet left on the following morning, stopping at sundown, twenty-five miles above Napoleon, Ark.— Leaving early the next day, we arrived at Milliken's Bend, La., early on Christmas morning, where we remained until the first brigade destroyed the Shreveport & Texas R. R.

Our next point was Vicksburg, which is located at the upper end of one of the great bends of the Mississippi river, on the south-east bank. It is situated on very high bluffs, which would almost bar a direct attack from the front. The hills extend north-east to Haines' Bluff, on the Yazoo river, about ten miles above where it empties into the Mississippi. Between these hills and the two rivers are the Yazoo Swamps, noted for their dense woods and low, marshy lands, part of which was once the old bed of the Yazoo.

On the 26th we proceeded down the Mississippi to the mouth of the Yazoo, and up that river about six miles, where we landed on the south bank, on the 27th, with two days' rations, and bivouacked for the night on the river bank. During the evening we received orders to move on the following morning (Sunday) at four o'clock. We were on the march with our brigade at the appointed time. After following up the Yazoo two or three miles, we turned to the right, and marched several miles through a thick-timbered swamp. At about 8 A. M. the booming of cannon and the crash of musketry on our left told us the battle had begun.— We formed in line of battle, marched to the left of the road and halted. The fighting on our left increased with every volley. The smoke and fog became so thick we could scarcely see twenty yards in advance. We remained there a short time, when we were ordered forward, and after passing the troops in reserve, we soon reached the skirmish line of the 77th Ills. We then advanced with them in line of battle, through a dense forest of live-oak and cypress, covered with Spanish moss. We drove the enemy's pickets about a mile, when we came in sight of their fortifications, situated on a high hill, in front of which they had cut down the timber. We remained in sight of their batteries until evening, when the Regiment returned to the Division, about one mile in the rear, and camped for the night, leaving the 77th Ills. on picket.

The battle on our left continued without any intermission all day. The next day, 29th, at daybreak, the firing was resumed on our left, and was kept up as on the previous day. We remained in reserve until evening, when two companies were ordered on picket in the rear. That evening a heavy rain set in and continued all night. The day following being too wet for military operations, we remained in camp.

Dec. 31st, the Regiment went on picket, occupying the position the 77th Ills. held on the 28th, with the right of the Regiment extending to the Mississippi river above Vicksburg. We relieved the old guards at 9 A. M. under a heavy fire. We spent a quiet day, except an occasional shot from the rebel pickets. That night we suffered from the cold weather, having left everything but our rubber blankets on the boat. In the absence of woolen blankets, the pickets in reserve made beds out of Spanish moss.

January 1st, 1863, we were relieved, and returned to camp in the rear again. New Year's day was spent in making shelter, gathering leaves and moss for beds, and cleaning our camp-ground. But we were not permitted to enjoy our comfortable booths. At 9 o'clock that evening, Companies C and K were sent to the landing, with orders to load all our stores by 4 o'clock next morning on board the steamer "City of Alton," as the army was to evacuate at that time. We labored hard all night, and at daylight the troops embarked on the boats, but the fleet did not leave until 1 o'clock P. M. Shortly after leaving, a violent rain-storm began and raged two days and nights. What our condition would have been had we remained in that dismal swamp, called by the soldiers "the valley of death," can better be imagined than described.

The campaign contemplated an attack on Vicksburg, by Gen. Grant's army marching through Mississippi from Memphis, and getting in the rear of Vicksburg, while Gen. Sherman, with 40,000 men, was to descend the Mississippi river, and attack from the north, on Chickasaw Bayou. But the day before Gen. Sherman left Memphis with his fleet, Holly Springs, Gen. Grant's base of supplies, with its immense quantity of military stores, had surrendered to the rebels without firing a shot, which compelled Gen. Grant to retreat. Gen. Sherman not being aware of this, made the attack alone. The enemy then sent their troops by rail to Vicksburg in such numbers that they soon outnumbered us. They being behind fortifications, had every advantage, which made it an unequal contest. After a loss of about 2,000 men, Gen. Sherman withdrew his army, and on the 4th of January, 1863, was relieved by Gen. McClernand, who assumed command and divided the army into two corps. Gen. Morgan commanded the first corps,

to which our Division — A. J. Smith's — belonged.
This Division afterward became the 13th Corps,
and Gen. Sherman was placed in command of the
second Corps.

Gen. McClernand soon after ordered the army
to Arkansas Post. We now proceeded up the Mississippi with the fleet, arriving at the mouth of
White river during the night of the 7th of January.
We remained until the 9th, then started up White
river. Upon reaching the cut-off, we crossed to
the Arkansas, and passed up that river to within
three miles of Arkansas Post, and tied up on the
right bank at 10 o'clock A. M., Jan. 10th. The
troops disembarked, with two days rations, and at
3 P. M. we started up the river. After marching
an hour, we halted in a corn-field, and after partaking of a hasty supper, we resumed our march.
In the meantime the gun-boats had opened a
heavy fire on the rebel batteries, in the fort, which
was continued for several hours without intermission. After passing the gun-boats, that lay in the
bend of the river, just below, and in range of the
rebel batteries, we entered a dense swamp. Night
overtook us and then our march became difficult.
Passing over logs, through mud and water, we
halted at 9 P. M., in the rear of the rebel fort, and
slept on our arms. The weather was cold, and being
without blankets, and allowed no fires, we spent a
very disagreeable night.

Sunday morning, Jan. 11th, our brigade was ordered to a position on the extreme left, within sight of the fort, and a few hundred yards from the river. Here we remained until 11 o'clock A. M., when, with two other regiments of the brigade, we were ordered back to the center of the Division, in reserve. At half-past twelve, the batteries being in position, opened, with the gunboats, a terrific cannonading, which continued half an hour before the infantry became engaged. We were then ordered to the right to support Gen. Burbridge's brigade. Here we left our haversacks and blankets, and advanced in the direction of the fort. Upon reaching the edge of the woods, we were halted.

We were now within reach of the enemy's fire, and now and then a shell would come crashing through the timber. Before us was a large, open field ; on the opposite side, the rebel fort ; to our right, their entrenchments. Half-way across the field was the first line of our infantry, fiercely engaged. We had halted but a few minutes, when Gen. A. J. Smith ordered us to the right. We had proceeded but a short distance, when some of the troops in front were thrown into confusion. At that moment Maj. Hammond, of Gen. Sherman's staff, came riding up and gave the command, "48th Ohio, by the left flank, double-quick, *march !*" This put us in line of battle, facing the enemy. With a wild cheer, we started across the field, halting within twenty yards of the first line of battle, occupied at that point by the 23d Wisconsin.— We were halted and ordered to lie down, when we were informed that Col. Parker had been wounded in the arm, and that Capt. Peterson, of Co. K, was in command of the Regiment.

We remained here about fifteen minutes, when we moved forward and relieved the 23d Wisconsin, who were out of ammunition. This brought us within one hundred yards of the fort, and a field battery, just outside. This battery, and also one of steel guns, on the inside of the fort, were soon silenced by our unerring fire. Our batteries, which had been brought up, soon exploded the enemy's magazines and caissons, which sent the fragments flying to every part of their works. The gun-boats, having disabled the two large siege guns, that commanded their approach, passed the fort, and poured broadside after broadside into the enemy's rear.

The long lines of our infantry that stretched away to the right, had advanced under a heavy fire from the enemy, to within a short distance of their entrenchments, and were preparing for a charge, when the rebels, at 20 minutes past 4 P. M., raised the white flag. With a loud cheer, we started on double-quick to the fort. Our Regiment was among the first to enter, and our flag was the second planted on the rebel fortifications. Three of our companies were commanded by First Sergeants. The Regiment lost two killed and thirteen wounded.

The army captured about 5,000 rebel prisoners and all their military supplies. That night, we bivouacked on the battle-ground, and on the following day, after destroying the fortifications, we camped in the woods, a short distance below the fort.

Jan. 14th, the Regiment was ordered on board the "City of Alton," and one company on picket. It rained all day, and continued until midnight, when it turned to snow. The pickets suffered more from exposure that night, than at any other time during their entire service.

CHAPTER IX.

Return Down the River — Napoleon — Young's Point — Digging the Canal — Overflowed — Scheme Abandoned — Pioneer Corps — Promotions — Arrival of General Grant — New Camp — Milliken's Bend — Change of Surgeons — Paymaster — Complimentary Order — Major Moats — Military Board — Seventeenth Ohio Battery.

WE left Arkansas Post on the morning of Jan. 17th, and arrived at Napoleon at noon, where we remained Sunday, the 18th. During that night three of the Regiment deserted. The next day we started for Young's Point, situated opposite Vicksburg, where we arrived on the 21st.

Our trips on steamboats were very unhealthy, especially when confined any length of time, with so large a number as we had on the "City of Alton." The 48th was put on with the 108th Illinois, that had over 1,000 men, besides Col. Landrum's brigade headquarters, and all the horses and mules belonging to the two regiments. In pleasant weather the men could sleep comfortably almost anywhere, but during a rain or snow-storm the suffering from exposure was intense.

The army was compelled to live principally on crackers, as there were no accommodations whatever for cooking. Before leaving Arkansas Post the weather turned very cold, which, with the unavoidable use of the Yazoo water at Vicksburg, the close confinement on the over-crowded steamboats, and poorly prepared food, disabled nearly half the troops in the whole expedition. The 108th Illinois, being a new regiment, suffered severely. Nearly three-fourths were rendered unable for duty, and death was thinning their ranks at a fearful rate, so that our steamer had the appearance of a hospital boat. Our Regiment escaped with scarcely any sickness, especially of a fatal character.

January 14th, Capt. John W. Frazee resigned, and on the 23d, First Lieut. Charles A. Partridge's resignation was accepted. The same day we disembarked, and marched three miles down the river, and camped along the levee. On the 25th, the Regiment was allotted its share of the canal. Our portion was the length of the Regiment, as it stood in two ranks.

Jan. 26th, a detail of eight men from the Regiment was made for the gun-boat Chillicothe. In the attack on Fort Pemberton, March 12th, 1863, while the Chillicothe was shelling the fort, a shell from the enemy exploded at the port-hole, just as our gunners were in the act of loading, which exploded their shell, aud killed Thomas Henderson, of company D, wounded a member of company K, and J. F. Holladay, of company C, in the right foot, which made amputation necessary.

Our time was occupied in digging the canal across the bend of the river. Our part was completed on the 6th of February. Some of the other regiments, however, were not so far advanced, when the river, which had been rising, broke over the dam at the levee that night, and flooded the whole peninsula with from five to seven feet of water, which caused the scheme to be abandoned.

The object of the canal was to let the boats pass through, and thus avoid the batteries in front of Vicksburg. Since the close of the war, a channel has been cut across the point where the first attempt to dig the canal by dredge-boats was made, and boats are now obliged to pass through this channel, which in time will leave Vicksburg off at one side.

On the 6th of February, the Pioneer Corps was organized, by transfers from each regiment in the brigade. The 48th furnished fifteen men as its quota.

Feb. 14th, Capt. Robins resigned; on the 15th, Capt. Joshua Hussey; on the 20th, Capt. J. C. Kelsey; and on the 21st, Capt. S. G. W. Peterson and Lieut. W. E. Brayman, Quartermaster. Lieut. J. R. Lynch was appointed Quartermaster in the latter's place.

Young's Point, at that time of the year, presented a dark and gloomy aspect. In our front was the Mississippi river; in the rear, a dreary swamp, covered with water, from one to two feet deep, leaving us but a narrow strip of dry land along the levee, on which to set our tents. The winter winds and heavy rains had unobstructed play on our canvas dwellings, and it was a common occurrence for the men to emerge from underneath their prostrate tents, after a heavy storm of wind and rain, as it swept down the Mississippi.

On the 18th, the following commissions were received from Gov. Tod: J. C. Kelsey, J. A. Bering, Joshua Hussey and R. T. Wilson, promoted to Captains. C. P. Bratt, Geo. W. Mosgrove, Daniel Gunsaullus and J. R. Lynch to First Lieutenants; Cornelius Conard, Thomas Montgomery and M. McCafferty to Second Lieutenants. In the meantime, Gen. Grant had arrived and taken command, and reorganized the whole army. Our Brigade and Division was placed in the 13th Army Corps, under Gen. McClernand.

Feb. 20th, we moved a short distance up the river, to a higher camping-ground. The river still kept rising, therefore, March 9th, the Regiment embarked on the steamer "Hiawatha," and moved up with our Corps to Milliken's Bend, La., and camped along the levee.

March 11th, Surgeon M. F. Carey, who had been captured at Shiloh, having resigned after he was exchanged, Ass't. Surgeon Plyn. A. Willis was promoted to Surgeon. A. A. Johnson, our Ass't. Surgeon, who had remained with the Regiment when scarcely able to stand, and neglected himself while attending to the duties of the hospital, and part of the time all alone, was finally compelled to resign. He took his departure when we left Young's Point.

March 14th, we received four months pay, and sent our surplus money home by Rev John Spence, our Chaplain, who resigned on the 18th. The same day, Serg't. Major E. A. Conkling was discharged on account of disability. On the 28th, we were inspected by the Corps-officer of the day, and on the next day the following order was issued, in regard to our camp, and read to the troops on dress-parade :

"HEADQUARTERS 13TH ARMY CORPS, }
MILLIKEN'S BEND, LA., March 29, 1863. }
"Accepting the report of the Corps-officer of the day as a tribute to merit, the Commanding General, John A. McClernand, takes great pleasure in commending the cleanliness and good government which characterizes the camps of the 48th and 114th Ohio Infantry, as being worthy of imitation.
[Signed] "Your Ob't Serv't. &c.,
"WALTER B. SCATES,
"Lieut. Col. & Ass't. Adj't. Gen'l.
"To 48th Ohio, through Gen. A. J. Smith."

The praise received for the cleanliness and good order of our camp, on this as well as other occasions, was in a great measure due to the untiring energy of Adj't. McGill.

April 2d, one hundred and fifteen men and two officers were sent as a guard, with a boat that was used by a military board, in collecting evidence along the Mississippi river, in regard to some cotton speculations. They were absent one week, during which time the remainder of the Regiment was excused from duty. While here a detail of ten men was made from the Regiment to fill up the 17th Ohio Battery.

Since leaving Memphis, the Regiment had lost by resignation fifteen officers. Their places had been partly filled by promotions in February. On the 9th of April, Capt. Moats returned from Columbus, Ohio, promoted to Major, and took command of the Regiment. He brought commissions for the following members of the Regiment: D. Gunsaullus, promoted to Captain; A. M. Cochran, C. Conard, Thomas Montgomery, W. H. H. Rike, M. McCafferty, W. H. Smith and R. A. South to First Lieutenants; and Harvey W. Day, J. K. Reed, J. M. Kendall, Jesse H. Allison and W. J. Srofe to Second Lieutenants. Shortly after, Lieut. Conard, Co. A, and Lieut. Plyly, Co. B, were permanently transferred to the Signal Corps, and Lieut. Jesse H. Allison was detailed as Aid-de-Camp on the staff of Col. W. J. Landrum.

While at Milliken's Bend, the sickness contracted on steamers and at Young's Point began to terminate fatally, the mortality being confined chiefly to the new regiments. The muffled drums were heard all day long, and the parting volleys at the graves on the slope of the levee awoke the echoes across the waters of the Mississippi, while comrades were laid in their last resting-place, far from the loved ones at home.

"Soldier, rest! thy warfare o'er;
Dream of battle-fields no more;
Sleep the sleep that knows not breaking,
Morn of toil, nor night of waking."

CHAPTER X.

Marching Orders — To the Rear of Vicksburg — Holmes' Plantation — Our Gun-boats Passing the Vicksburg Batteries — Smith's Landing — Return of Lieut. Col. Parker — Lake St. Joe — Grand Gulf — Crossing the Mississippi at Bruinsburg — Battle of Magnolia Hills — Port Gibson — Grind-Stone Ford — Foragers — Rocky Springs — Willow Springs — Cayuga — Gen. Sherman's Visit — Old Auburn — Raymond — Battle of Champion Hills — Black River Bridge.

APRIL 15th, we received marching orders, and left with the Corps on our way through Louisiana, to the rear of Vicksburg. The troops, as usual on the first day's march in a campaign, loaded themselves down with extra clothing, blankets and surplus baggage. The day proved to be one of those hot, sultry, spring days, with not a ripple of air stirring. At the first halt, knapsacks were unloaded, which process continued all day. By night the army was in light marching order. The line of march had been strewn with abandoned clothing, &c., which the slaves gathered as we passed. We camped near Richmond, La., at sun-down; continued our march the next day and camped in the evening at Holmes' Plantation, Madison Parish. During the night the gun-boats and transports ran past the batteries at Vicksburg. Gen. Sherman, in his "Memoirs," gives a graphic description of the passage of the boats past the batteries. He says:

"Gen. Grant's orders for the general movement past Vicksburg by Richmond and Carthage, were dated April 20, 1863. McClernand was to lead off with his corps, McPherson next, and my corps (the 15th) to bring up the rear. Preliminary thereto, on the night of April 16, seven iron-clads, led by Admiral Porter in person, in the Benton, with three transports and ten barges in tow, ran the Vicksburg batteries by night. Anticipating a scene, I had four yawl-boats hauled across the swamp to the reach of the river below Vicksburg, and manned them with soldiers, ready to pick up any of the disabled wrecks as they floated by. I was out on the stream when the fleet passed Vicksburg, and the scene was truly sublime. As soon as the rebel gunners detected the Benton, which was in the lead, they opened on her, and on the others in succession, with shot and shell. Houses on the Vicksburg side and on the opposite shore were set on fire, which lighted up the whole river; and the roar of cannon, bursting of shells, and finally the burning of the Henry Clay, drifting with the current, made up a picture terrible, not often seen. Each gun-boat returned the fire as she passed the town, while the transports hugged the opposite shore.

"When the Benton had got abreast of us, I pulled off to her, boarded, and had a few words with Admiral Porter, and as she was drifting rapidly toward the batteries at Warrenton, I left, and pulled back toward the shore, meeting the gunboat Tuscumbia, towing the Forest Queen into the bank, out of the range of fire. The Forest Queen, Capt. Conway, had been my flag-boat up the Arkansas, and for some time after, and I was very friendly with the officers. This was the only transport whose Captain would not receive volunteers as a crew, but her own officers and crew carried her safely below the Vicksburg batteries, and afterward rendered splendid service in ferrying troops across the river at Grand Gulf and Bruinsburg. In passing Vicksburg she was damaged in the hull, and had a steam-pipe cut away, but this was soon repaired. The Henry Clay was set on fire by bursting shells, and burned up. One of my yawls picked up her pilot, floating on a piece of wreck, and the bulk of her crew escaped in their own yawl-boat to the shore above. The Silver Wave, Capt. McMillan, the same that was with us up Steel's Bayou, passed safely, and she rendered good service afterward.

"Subsequently, on the night of April 26th, six other transports, with numerous barges loaded with hay, corn, freight and provisions, were drifted past Vicksburg. Of these the Tigress was hit, and sunk just as she reached the river bank below, on our side. I was there with my yawls, and saw Col. Lagow, of Gen. Grant's staff, who had passed the batteries on the Tigress, and I think he was satisfied never to attempt such a thing again. Thus Gen. Grant's army had below Vicksburg an abundance of stores, and boats with which to cross the river."

We remained here until the 24th, when at 8 o'clock P. M. we received orders to march in fifteen minutes, at which time it began to rain. In half an hour we were on the road, which was rough and slippery, and through a soil of black loam that had been badly cut up by the advance troops. The night being very dark, we made slow progress through the mud and rain. We halted at three o'clock next morning in a corn-field, at Smith's Landing, near Carthage. Here we were allowed but one wagon to the Regiment, and all the extra baggage was left behind.

On the 26th, Lieut. Col. Parker, who had been home since he was wounded at the battle of Arkansas Post, returned and took command of the Regiment. Resumed our march that evening at 7 o'clock, in the rain, and halted near midnight, on the road-side. We continued our march the next day, but owing to the rain and bad roads, we made but four miles. On the 28th, we reached the Mississippi river at noon, marched down the levee, and struck Lake St. Joe. On the banks of this delightful lake were beautiful mansions, with lawns, surrounded by hedge-roses in full bloom, which was a great contrast to the country through which we had passed. The high state of cultivation of the plantations, with the droves of slaves, indicated that the war had reached the homes of the wealthy people of the South.

On the 29th, we reached the Mississippi river again, and camped opposite Grand Gulf. That night seven gun-boats and six transports, under a heavy fire, and in full view of the army, ran past the rebel batteries. The next day, April 30th, at 1 P. M., the 48th Ohio and 77th Illinois, leaving wagons and all baggage behind, embarked on the U. S. gun-boat Louisville, of which Acting Ensign Frank Bates was the executive officer, and landed ten miles below, at Bruinsburg, Mississippi. We remained there until 11 o'clock that night, when we moved forward with the army to Port Gibson. We marched all night, and on account of the heavy firing in front, did not halt for breakfast in the morning, but hastened forward on double-quick until 10 o'clock A. M., when we reached the battle-field of Magnolia Hills, near Port Gibson. This name was derived from the magnolia trees, which were in full bloom.

We crossed an open field and entered a thick cane-brake, through which we penetrated in line of battle, with great difficulty. We were now in range of the enemy's fire, and their musket-balls came crashing through the cane thick and fast. Just as we emerged from the cane-brake into an open field, the enemy repulsed an Iowa regiment. We hurried to their assistance, which caused the enemy to retreat We made a halt on the crest of a hill, in full view of the rebel army, who still held a very strong position on our right, but they, fearing a flank movement, withdrew in haste.

We bivouacked on the battle-field, and during the night our supplies reached us. Rations were issued for supper, making the first meal that day. The long roll beat about midnight, but proved to be a false alarm. The only casualty in our Regiment was one wounded in Co. K. The enemy's fire was too high, cutting off the cane far above our heads. Early next morning, May 2d, we advanced with a strong skirmish-line in front, and entered Port Gibson at 9 A. M., where we found the public and private buildings crowded with rebel wounded. The Regiment stacked arms on the side-walk, under the shade-trees. The enemy had retreated over the south fork of Piere river, destroying the bridge after them. The following morning we crossed the river on a pontoon bridge, marched all day, and crossed the north fork at Grindstone Ford in the evening, and camped near the stream.

The provisions that we started with had lasted up to this time, but we had cut loose from our base, which prevented us from getting another supply. Orders were therefore issued to subsist on the products of the country through which we marched; and from that time forward until the siege of Vicksburg, foraging parties, or perhaps better known as "bummers," were sent out daily, to procure all the provisions and forage that was required for the army. They left camp every morning, in advance of the infantry, and a curious sight they were to behold, as they galloped by at full speed, mounted on such "critters" as they could gather up on their expeditions. They were dressed in such clothes as suited their fancy—the Union blue, the rebel gray and butternut, with a considerable number in citizens' attire.

They were a jolly, mischievous set, eager and ready for any adventure. No sooner were they beyond the lines than they began their work. They slaughtered the pigs in the pens; the cattle and horses were driven from the fields; smokehouses and cellars were ransacked for flour, meal and bacon; the chickens and turkeys were captured in the yard; the mules were hitched to the family carriage, and the provisions stowed away in it, when it was driven to the next plantation, where the same ceremony was repeated. Toward evening the foragers returned to camp, driving the cattle before them, followed by a long line of vehicles of every description, loaded with all kinds of provisions, which was equally distributed among the different regiments.

We remained at Grindstone Ford until May 5th, when the Regiment was detailed to guard Gen. McClernand's headquarters. In the evening we resumed our march, and halted at midnight at Rocky Springs. We remained here until the 8th, when, by request of Col. W. J. Landrum, our brigade commander, we were relieved and joined our brigade at Willow Springs. We left that evening, and camped at Cayuga the next evening. The following day, May 11th, Gen. Sherman's Corps arrived. While his troops were passing, he paid us a friendly visit, and discussed the campaign quite familiarly with the Regiment. He also said, he would be pleased to have us back again in his Corps. When he took his departure, three rousing cheers were given for Gen. Sherman, the favorite of the 48th.

We left May 12th, and camped the day following at Old Auburn, where we remained until the 15th, when we left for Raymond, arriving there in the evening, and camped near the battle-field of the 12th. On the morning of the 16th, the 48th Ohio and 19th Ky. were ordered to guard the Division train. The enemy was now contending for every foot of advantageous ground, which made our advance very slow. At 11 A. M. they made a bold stand with 25,000 men, at Champion Hills, a very strong position. Our troops were now hurried forward. The artillery passed us on a gallop. Regiment after regiment went by on the double-quick, covered with dust, which told plainly of many miles traveled that morning. We were still guarding the train, but when the battle commenced we were relieved by request of Lieut. Col. Parker and sent to our Division, on the extreme left, and placed in the reserve. By 2 o'clock P. M. Gen. Hovey had made several unsuccessful attempts to drive the enemy from his position, but was repulsed with a heavy loss. In the meantime, our Corps on the left, and Gen. Logan on the right, were swinging around to their rear. Gen. Logan, reaching their exposed point first, made a sudden attack, in which the rebels lost heavily in killed and wounded, and one entire brigade was taken prisoners. Their whole line wavered, then fled in disorder to the fortifications at Big Black. Our army lost in killed and wounded 2,500 men, the rebel loss being about the same. The enemy was pursued until dark, and on the following morning the army advanced and found the rebels behind their works, at Black River Bridge.

The enemy had already been defeated on four battle-fields of their own selection ; but now they were behind their fortifications, and firmly believed they could not be driven farther. After some brisk skirmishing the troops were placed in position. Our Division occupied the extreme left. When the command was given for the assault, the movement was executed so suddenly that our forces were in the enemy's works before they could realize their situation, capturing 18 pieces of artillery and 1,800 prisoners. The rest fled, badly demoralized, to Vicksburg. During the day we found the country full of rebels, who had been separated from their commands in the rout. Our Regiment captured quite a number, and turned them over to the 108th Ills. that evening at Black River Bridge.

We camped that night inside the fortifications. One company was sent on picket on the extreme left of our line. The two armies having been so near each other since the 15th, the foragers did not have an opportunity to collect supplies sufficient for the whole army; therefore the Regiment was compelled to eat parched corn for breakfast the next morning.

As soon as the pontoon over Black river was completed, our brigade crossed and took the advance of the army, camping that evening within seven miles of Vicksburg. On all sides the evidences of the complete rout and panic of the enemy were to be seen—abandoned camps, baggage, artillery wagons, ammunition, and arms of every description, lined the road. This was one of the most exciting periods of our service; fighting by day and marching at night, and resting only when the road became obstructed with troops or wagon-trains. From early morning until late at night the rattle of musketry and roar of artillery was heard, while the enemy was being forced back from every point. But the romance of this was soon to pass away, and the rather monotonous work of digging rifle-pits and building fortifications was to commence.

CHAPTER XI.

SIEGE OF VICKSBURG.

Assault on the Nineteenth — Attack on the Twentieth — Charge on the Twenty-Second — Our Flag on the Rebel Fort — Retreat After Night — Killed and Wounded — Extract from Cincinnati Commercial — Flag of Truce — Burying the Dead — Picketing and Mining — Blowing Up of Fort Hill—Surrender of Vicksburg, July 4th.

N the morning of May 19th, we advanced again, and after a two hours' march, over a very rugged and hilly country, we came in sight of Vicksburg, which is built on a series of high bluffs, and contained 10,000 inhabitants. The defenses of the city consisted of a chain of forts, at intervals of 800 yards, for a distance of seven miles, both right and left, resting on the Mississippi river, and forming a semi-circle around the city. The rifle pits filled the intervals between the forts. In front of these was a ditch fifteen feet wide and ten feet deep. The works were more formidable than we expected to find them, showing that they were fully prepared to receive us.

As soon as the enemy discovered us advancing over the hills, they opened on us with their artillery. Our batteries were hurried forward into position, and under their fire we advanced a short distance and halted in a ravine. At 10 A. M., Gen. A. J. Smith ordered all the officers of the Regiment to report at his headquarters. On arriving there, he told them to inform their men that at 2 o'clock P. M. we would storm the rebel works. The news was received by the Regiment in a quiet and serious manner, and the suspense until 2 o'clock was somewhat like that of the culprit awaiting the hour of his execution. Promptly at the hour the signal-gun was fired, and the order came, "Forward, 48th!" We started up the hill, and on reaching the summit we were greeted with shot and shell from the rebel forts; but without faltering, on we went, down into the next ravine, through brush and over fallen trees. Arriving at the foot of a hill, we continued up the narrow valley under the guns of the fort, and drove the rebel outposts into their fortifications, when a halt was ordered, to allow the troops to join us on the left. By the time they made the connection the sun was setting in the west. Our opportunity for taking Vicksburg that day had passed, and we bivouacked for the night.

May 20th, we remained there until 3 P. M., when we moved to the left of our Division. On arriving there, we were ordered across an open field to gain a strong position behind a bluff, still nearer to the rebel works. We went over the field on double-quick, one company at a time, in full range of their artillery and infantry fire. The movement was very successfully executed, and our loss was one color-guard mortally wounded. Adjutant McGill made a narrow escape, with a ball through his cap. From this position we returned the enemy's fire with considerable effect. At 9 P. M. we were relieved by the 11th Wisconsin, and returned to the rear.

The next day, May 21st, was employed in long-range artillery practice and maneuvering for advantageous positions.

May 22d, orders were issued for a general assault along the lines at 11 o'clock A. M. The echo of the signal-gun had scarcely died away, when our brigade was ordered forward to take the fort in our front, situated on a hill, in an angle of their intrenchments, where their guns commanded every approach. Down the ravine we started on double-quick, checking our speed for a moment in a deep gully, to reform our line before facing the fort, whose incessant fire shook the ground at every discharge. Then on we went, up the hill, through the brush and undergrowth, but did not check our speed until the right of the Regiment, in conjunction with the left of the 77th Illinois, reached the fort. Leaping into the ditch, and climbing the parapet, the colors of the 48th Ohio and 77th Illinois were planted on the fort. The rebel gunners surrendered and were hurried to the rear. During this charge Major Moats was mortally wounded in the knee.

We were now exposed to an enfilading fire from the right and left, which was thinning our ranks at a fearful rate. We were left there to contend against great odds, without any assistance whatever. At 4 P. M. the rebels massed their troops on our front, and attacked us with great fury, and re-took the fort, capturing the colors and fifty men of the 77th Ills. Ike Carmin, one of our colorguards, with a bayonet-wound in the leg, clung to our flag and saved it from sharing the same fate. This was the signal for a second attack on both sides. Another charge was ordered all along the line. It was a glorious sight to see our troops advancing in plain view over the hills, to our assistance. But as soon as they got within range of the rebel fire, they were mown down and almost annihilated. So destructive was the concentrated fire of the enemy, that not a single man of those sent to reinforce us reached our line. In the meantime, a few spades and shovels had been brought up, with which the Regiment hastily threw up rude entrenchments, from which they kept up an unceasing fire until dark, when the firing ceased and all became quiet. We remained on the battle-field until the town clock in Vicksburg struck the hour of 10 P. M., when we were ordered to retreat, which we accomplished without being discovered by the enemy. Before the engagement commenced, stretcher-bearers were detailed to carry the wounded of the Regiment off the battle-field. They succeeded in removing all the wounded to the rear.

When we retreated we attempted to carry off

our dead, but on account of the darkness and the rugged nature of the locality, we had to abandon the undertaking, and leave them where they fell.

The following is an extract from the Cincinnati Commercial, of June 1st, 1863:

"On the left, Gen. McClernand commenced the assault earlier than any other commander. The first advance was made by McClernand's center, Gen. A. J. Smith's Divison of two brigades, commanded by Col. Landrum and Gen. Burbridge. As early as 11 o'clock Col. Landrum's men took a fort, and were in actual possession of it. Gen. Osterhouse, on their left, made a breach in the south side of the works, with his artillery. There were two companies of rebel soldiers in it at the time. One of them ran away, and the other actually burrowed their way through the earth to our men in front, and surrendered as prisoners. Landrum, on obtaining possession of the fort, put a pioneer force at work to throw up earth-works in the rear, so as to bring the guns of the fort to bear upon the rebels. In constructing the fortifications, the rebels left the rear of all the forts open, to give them an opportunity to assail our men, in the event of our success in driving them out. The flags of the 48th Ohio, 77th Illinois and 19th Ky. floated from the inner slope of the parapet from half-past 11 A. M. till 4 P. M. At the latter hour the rebels were seen preparing for a charge, to re-take the fort. An entire brigade was about to be pitted against a few companies. Our men did not receive the support which had been promised them, and were compelled to fall back, leaving the enemy again in possession of the fort. The 48th Ohio acquitted itself very creditably in the affair. The conduct of its officers and men is highly spoken of. I enclose a list of the casualties of the Regiment. * * *

"List of killed and wounded, 48th Ohio : Lieut. Col. Parker, wounded in the face with rifle ball; Maj. V. H. Moats, wounded in leg ; Co. A, Serg't. John Yost, killed; Alonzo Smith, killed ; Mahlon Davis, killed ; David Woosley, wounded dangerously ; Isaac McPherson, wounded dangerously; Isaac Carmin, wounded severely; Co. B, John Cooper, wounded dangerously; Isaac Scott, wounded dangerously; Co. C, Serg't. Charles Weber, killed; Serg't. J. D. Leonard, wounded slightly; Corp. Sam'l Hair, wounded slightly; George Pfister, wounded severely; L. A. Williams, wounded mortally; Co. D, Joseph Balon, killed; Serg't. John Wilson, wounded slightly ; Co. E, Carl Hough, wounded severely ; Henry Stitchter, wounded severely; Co. F, Lewis Farris, wounded dangerously; John Kead, wounded severely ; Thos. O'Borke, wounded severely ; Co. G, Serg't. James Sweet, killed ; Peter A. Deler, wounded in the head ; Co. H, Jacob Davidson, wounded severely ; Co. I, Elliott J. Bich, killed ; John W. Hubbard, killed ; Chris. O. Sroffe, killed ; Co. K, Elias Conover, wounded slightly ; Henry Knob, wounded slightly; W. A. Chaffin, killed. * * * Total, ten killed and twenty-five wounded. MACK."

The work entitled, "The Battles for the Union," in giving an account of that charge, says:

"The colors of the 48th Ohio and 77th Illinois were placed on the bastion, and within the next quarter of an hour the brigade of Benton and Burbridge, fired by this example, had carried the ditch of another strong earthwork, while Capt. White, of the Chicago Mercantile Battery, carried forward one of his guns by hand to the ditch, double shotted it and fired into the embrasures."

Gen. Sherman, in his "Memoirs," says:

"The two several assaults made May 22d, on the lines of Vicksburg, had failed, by reason of the great strength of the position, and the determined fighting of its garrison. I have since seen the position of Sevastopol, and without hesitation, I declare that at Vicksburg to have been the more difficult of the two."

May 23d, we occupied our old camp, and but few shots were exchanged between the two armies until the 25th, when the rebels agreed to cease hostilities for two hours in order to permit us to bury our dead and remove our wounded, some of whom were left on the battle-field where they fell. During the truce we proceeded to the position occupied by our Regiment during the assault. The rebel Colonel, in command of the fort on which we planted our flag on the 22d, informed Col. Parker that they had buried all the dead in that vicinity. The battle-field presented a ghastly sight. The dead lay thick, in every conceivable position, on the hill-side beneath the rebel intrenchments. Some of the wounded were still alive, but in a terrible condition, having lain between the contending armies for three days without food, water or medical attention. After the burial parties had performed their sad task, we withdrew from the field, and the firing was resumed on both sides.

Our army lost on the 22d, 3,000 killed and wounded, and nothing accomplished. Gen. Grant became convinced by this time that Vicksburg was too strong to be taken by assault, and therefore wisely concluded to lay a regular siege. The troops were encamped in the numerous ravines. Our Regiment was in a ravine near the R. R. bridge, and within reach of the enemy's guns, but the hills protected us from their direct fire. Nevertheless, stray shots were too numerous to be comfortable. Several men were wounded in their tents, but none fatally in our Regiment.

Our duty was to dig and man one of the rifle-pits, which was within one hundred yards of one of their main forts. To approach these rifle-pits, tunnels were made through the hills, thus connecting the ravines. The details for pickets and for digging rifle-pits, were always sent to their posts and relieved very quietly during the night. In some places we succeeded in digging the rifle-pits to within a few feet of their fort, being protected from their musketry by large bundles of cane, that were kept in front while approaching, the enemy in the meantime trying to get possession of the cane by means of hooks attached to long poles, or destroying them by throwing turpentine-balls and setting them on fire, while our men in return would annoy them by throwing hand grenades and short-fuse shells into their fort, which usually elicited quite a spirited conversation between the combatants.

June 3d, Lieut.-Col. J. R. Parker, having received a leave of absence, went home, leaving Capt. Lindsey in command of the Regiment.— Shortly after, Col. Sullivan arrived and took command. June 22d, Lieut. J. H. Allison, A. D. C. on the staff of Col. Landrum, being sick, Lieut. Montgomery was detailed to take his place during the siege. On the 25th, Capt. F. M. Posegate, of Co. D, resigned.

Gen. McPherson, who had been undermining Fort Hill, had completed it by the 25th, and was then ready to blow up the fort. The troops were therefore placed in the advance rifle-pits, ready to rush into the breach and capture Vicksburg, should he be successful in blowing it up; but the explosion did not result in destroying the works to such an extent as to enable the troops to enter. After the explosion, we were ordered back to our camp.

Our duties were getting more arduous every day, besides being continually under fire, until July 3d, when Gen. Pemberton sent Gen. Bowen and Col. Montgomery, under a flag of truce, with a proposition for the surrender of Vicksburg. They were taken, with their eyes bandaged, to our brigade headquarters, and had a consultation with Gen. Grant, but he would not consent to anything but an unconditional surrender. Nevertheless, he agreed to hold a conference with Gen. Pemberton, to discuss the matter. Accordingly, they met under a tree, between the two armies, who had now ceased firing and were watching with great interest the movements of the Generals. The last proposition made by Gen. Grant was, that they should be paroled, the officers permitted to retain their side-arms and private property, and to stack their arms outside the fortifications. Gen. Pemberton withdrew to consult with his officers, and Gen. Grant issued an order to the troops "that the armistice should continue in force until 8 A. M., July 4th; then, if the enemy did not accept his terms, hostilities would be resumed." But on the morning of July 4th, before the time expired, they raised the white flag, and Vicksburg, after a campaign of over six months, and a siege of forty-eight days, with its immense fortifications, arms, munitions, and 37,000 prisoners, was ours. The entire rebel loss during the Vicksburg campaign in killed, wounded and prisoners, according to "Badeau," was 56,000.

The following vivid description of Vicksburg during the siege, is from the work, "The Battles for the Union:"

"Every day further progress was made in digging and mining, and at length a point was reached where the batteries could send their screaming shells directly to the heart of the city. A reign of terror took possession of the town, and its inhabitants dug themselves caves in the earth, seeking protection against the missiles of destruction which daily and nightly dropped in their midst. Such cannonading and shelling has perhaps scarcely been equaled. It was not safe from behind or before, and every part of the city was alike within range of the Federal guns. * * *

"Porter's gun-boats, with thirteen-inch mortars and one-hundred-pound Parrott guns, safely anchored under the high bank below Vicksburg, sentineled the river above and below. A three-gun battery, on the peninsula opposite, played havoc with the Confederate garrison, burning up their shot-and-shell foundry. While the enemy's forts were being mined, counter-mines were dug by them, and the sound of their picks could be heard through the thin wall of earth which separated the hostile armies.

"For six weeks our batteries never ceased dropping their shot and shell on the doomed city. Food became scarce, and the inhabitants grew wan and thin in their narrow dens. At last, despairing of Johnston's aid in raising the siege, and believing that Grant was ready for another assault on his works, they hung out the white flag in front of Gen. A. J. Smith's Division."

CHAPTER XII.

Marching Orders for Jackson — Excessive Heat — Siege of Jackson — Gen. Johnston Evacuates — Return to Vicksburg — Furloughs — Col. P. J. Sullivan Resigns — Steamer "City of Madison" Blown Up — Embarking for New Orleans — Camp at Carrollton — Grand Review by Gens. Grant and Banks — Extract from New Orleans Era.

WE had scarcely time that day to give vent to our joy at the surrender, before we were ordered to march in pursuit of Gen. Johnston, who was collecting quite an army at Jackson, Miss.

At daybreak on the morning of July 5th, we were on the march, and continued from day to day, under a sweltering July sun, until the 10th, when we reached the fortifications around Jackson. Our Regiment was then deployed as skirmishers, and advanced through the timber and bivouacked for the night. The following day we were ordered to the right, in support of the first brigade, where we remained during the siege, principally engaged in picket duty. On the morning of the 17th, we discovered that Gen. Johnston, after destroying his stores, had evacuated the preceding night. The loss of our Corps (13th) in killed and wounded was 760.

Gen. Sherman, who was in command of the

troops sent against Gen. Joe Johnston, gives the following account of the Jackson campaign :

"July 4th, Vicksburg surrendered, and orders were given for at once attacking Gen. Johnston. The 13th Corps (Gen. Ord) was ordered to march rapidly and cross the Big Black at the railroad bridge, the 15th by Messinger's, and the 9th (Gen. Parkes') by Birdsong's Ferry ; all to converge on Bolton. My corps crossed the Big Black during the 5th and 6th of July, and marched for Bolton, where we came in with Gen. Ord's troops, but the 9th Corps was delayed in crossing at Birdsong's. Johnston had received timely notice of Pemberton's surrender, and was in full retreat for Jackson. On the 8th, all our troops reached the neighborhood of Clinton, the weather fearfully hot, and water scarce. Johnston had marched rapidly, and in retreating had caused cattle, hogs and sheep to be driven into the ponds of water, and there shot down, so that we had to haul their dead carcases out to use the water. On the 10th of July we had driven the rebel army into Jackson, where it turned at bay behind the intrenchments, which had been enlarged and strengthened since our former visit in May. We closed our lines about Jackson; my corps (15th) held the center, extending from the Clinton to the Raymond road ; Ord's (13th) on the right, reaching Pearl River below the town; and Parkes' (9th) the left, above the town. On the 11th we pressed close in and shelled the town from every direction.

"One of Ord's brigades (Lauman's) got too close, and was very roughly handled and driven back in disorder. Gen. Ord accused the commander (Gen. Lauman) of having disregarded his orders, and attributed to him personally the disaster and heavy loss of men. He requested his relief, which I granted, and Gen. Lauman went to the rear, and never regained his division. * * *

"The weather was fearfully hot, but we continued to press the siege day and night, using our artillery pretty freely, and on the morning of July 17th, the place was found evacuated. Gen. Steele's division was sent in pursuit as far as Brandon, (fourteen miles), but Gen. Johnston had carried his army safely off, and pursuit in that hot weather would have been fatal to my command. Reporting the fact to Gen. Grant, he ordered me to return, to send Gen. Parkes' corps to Haines' Bluff, Gen. Ord's back to Vicksburg, and he consented that I should encamp my whole corps near the Big Black, pretty much on the same ground we had occupied before the movement, and with the prospect of a period of rest for the remainder of the summer. We reached our camps on the 27th of July."

On the 21st, we were ordered back to Vicksburg. We arrived at our old camp during the night of the 23d. The following day we marched through Vicksburg and camped one mile below, on the Mississippi river. Here we received our tents, having slept in the open air, exposed to the changeable weather, since April, which, together with short rations, being at times compelled to subsist on green corn alone, caused considerable sickness in the Regiment.

July 25th, we received notice that Major Moats had died on the 11th inst., from the effects of the wound received at the charge of the 22d of May. He was a brave, faithful and unassuming officer, and was held in high esteem by the whole Regiment.

We now resumed our daily routine of camp duty, that had been interrupted during the siege, which, after reveille, at daylight, consisted in attending roll-call; then followed guard-mounting and sick-call; after this, company drill until 11 A. M. In the afternoon we had battalion or brigade drill, and occasionally a "grand review," closing the day's exercises with dress-parade at sun-down, tattoo by the band at 9 o'clock, and "taps" at 10 P. M., when the guards ordered "lights out." Soon after, the Regiment was wrapped in slumber, as peaceful as though there was no war devastating the land. Thus the days slowly passed, while we lay broiling in the hot sun, in an open field, on the banks of the Mississippi.

After the siege, the Regiment received the Enfield Rifle in exchange for the old Austrian, which was a much better weapon for service, and we were well pleased with the change.

From one of the letters written home in August, 1863, we take the following:

"Yesterday I concluded to pay a visit to the Yazoo Swamps, where our army was during the unsuccessful attack on Vicksburg last December. Accordingly, after breakfast, I mounted my charger, and in an hour's ride I passed through Vicksburg and by all the upper river batteries. From there I descended into the valley, which we occupied last winter. After a careful survey of the ground which the rebels occupied, and that which was held by us, I have come to the conclusion that their position was as near impregnable as art and nature could make it. The swamps are as silent and dismal-looking as ever. The valley is covered with a rank growth of timber, underbrush and creeping vines. The limbs of the trees are covered with gray Spanish moss, that hangs in different lengths from every twig. It is this that gives it the air of solemnity, more than anything else. Add to this the rattle of musketry, the booming of cannon, a heavy rain, and then under cover of darkness to get out on double-quick, and leave on the boats for the Mississippi river, and last, but not least, to have it said that you are whipped, that Vicksburg *can't* be taken, then perhaps you can form a faint idea how we felt while going up the river, and why it was called 'The Valley of Death.'

"In one of my letters at that time I spoke of a solitary sentinel, who was standing guard before a battery of four siege-guns. That battery is still there, and a splendid one it is, but Mr. Reb. is missing. In his stead are two blue-coats, who, I think, will attend to the guns for some time to come. After a minute inspection of every ditch and battery on my route, I returned to camp, where I arrived in the afternoon, with my mind stored with zigzag ditches, breastworks, fortifications and numerous war implements."

While here, orders were given to issue thirty days' furlough to two men of each company; and all officers in excess of one to each company were granted thirty days leave of absence. Col. Sullivan, who had resigned on account of disability, produced by his wound received at Shiloh, in an appropriate speech bade the Regiment farewell, and left for home, August 9th, which left Capt. J. A. Bering in command. Lieut. Robt. McGill having also resigned, Lieut. R. A. South was appointed Adjutant, to fill the vacancy. On the 12th of August, Gen. E. O. C. Ord, who had superseded Gen. McClernand in command of the 13th Army Corps during the siege, was ordered to transfer his Corps to New Orleans, which severed our connection with the old "Army of the Tennessee," in which we had served since March 6th, 1862.

By this time, quite a number who had been absent for various causes, rejoined the Regiment. On the 19th, a detail of twenty men from the brigade was sent to load the steamer "City of Madison" with ammunition for our Corps, but a shell exploding, ignited the ammunition and blew the boat to atoms, killing and wounding quite a number, among the latter M. J. Grady, of Company A. The remainder of our Regiment escaped without injury.

A second detail was made, to load another steamer with the ammunition, which was put in charge of Lieut. Montgomery, who, after loading the boat, arrived with it at Carrollton, Aug. 31st.

On the 25th of August, the Regiment embarked for New Orleans on the steamer "Atlantic," with the 77th Ills. and Chicago Mercantile Battery, and arrived at Carrollton, five miles above New Orleans, on the 27th, and with the Division, in command of Gen. Burbridge, encamped in the old rebel camp "De Mar." Sept. 1st, Capt. Tice arrived and took command of the Regiment.

On the 9th, we moved our camp to Greenville Station, on the Carrollton & New Orleans R. R., in a beautiful grove of pecan trees. New Orleans had always been a city of great note for pleasure-seekers, and the war had made but little change in that respect. Therefore, as soon as we arrived at the Crescent City, enjoyment was the order of the day. During our stay, excursion parties were made up to visit the most notable places. This, with the very light duties required of us, made it one of the most pleasant periods of our service.

To the Northern soldier, New Orleans was very attractive, as it resembled more a foreign than an American city. The houses, especially in the suburbs, occupy a position back from the streets, in front of which are shrubbery and flowers. These, with the indispensable veranda, give the dwellings a cool and inviting look. The inhabitants, who are of French and Spanish descent, interest the stranger with their peculiar manners and customs.

The French market, on a Sunday morning, is an interesting scene. It is open until noon, and is thronged with customers. The stores are open until 11 A. M., when they close for the Sabbath, the observance of which consists principally in promenading on Canal street, which is said to be the finest street in America. It is very wide, and in the center runs a street railroad, on each side of which are beautiful shade trees, which form a complete arch over the track.

Cellars and wells are out of the question in this low, marshy soil, where water is found but a few feet from the surface. In fact, the city is lower than the Mississippi river at high water, and is only prevented from being overflowed by the levee. For the same reason the dead are buried in vaults, built above the ground. The principal cemetery is on the Shell Road, half-way between the city and Lake Ponchartrain. The Lake is a great public resort, for boating and fishing.

The old battle-field, below the city, received its full share of visitors. Here Gen. Jackson, on the 8th of January, 1812, with 4,000 raw recruits, defeated 12,000 British veterans, with a loss of only five men, while the British lost seven hundred. The most curious feature was, that it was fought after peace had been declared, but the combatants had not received the news. This was before railroads, steamers or the telegraph.

Gen. Grant having arrived, a "grand review" was ordered to take place on the 4th of September. The following is an editorial, taken from the New Orleans Era, giving an account of the review, in which the 48th Ohio took part:

[New Orleans Era, Saturday, Sept. 5, 1863.]

"THE REVIEW YESTERDAY.

"According to announcement in the city papers, the troops under command of Maj. Gen. Washburn, now stationed at 'Champ de Mars,' near Carrollton, were reviewed by Gens. Banks and Grant, at an early hour yesterday morning. The review was a most imposing sight, and one to be long remembered. The men under review were war-scarred veterans, who left the pleasant scenes of their homes in every part of the Union, to 'hew their way to the Gulf with their swords.' Every division, brigade and regiment, as it filed past the two Generals, surrounded by their staffs, showed the results of careful and skillful training, while the animation that gleamed from the bronzed faces of these veterans, gave evidence that they were conscious of the distinguished presence in which they were marching. In the array of officers and men who met together on the 'Champ de Mars,' the citizens of New Orleans could behold a portion of the deliverers of the Mississippi river. The opening of the great inland sea required great men and stout soldiers; and to the credit of our country let it be said, the right men were found for the work. *̣ * *

"The review was what might be reasonably expected from the tried troops, in the presence of the two distinguished Generals. The division, brigade and regimental officers handled their men with more precision than might have been witnessed on the same field two years ago, when an attempt was made by one or two Louisiana militia Generals to review raw recruits, who had never seen even a skirmish, and many of whom are still innocent of the blood of the soldiers of the army of the United States.

"The heat of the day was so intense, that many of the old citizens of New Orleans were glad to retire to some friendly shade; and yet the troops showed no signs of distress, nor even inconvenience. Such is the result of being inured to exposure. The men, coming from a northern climate, endure a heat which even an acclimated person avoids. A heartier or more robust set of men probably never passed in review under the critical eyes of Generals, who have performed great deeds, and who have more yet to do.

"It was apparent to the most superficial observer, that the parade was no training-day display. The two Generals, their respective staffs, the general field and regimental officers, and the men themselves, had the bearing of the true soldier, and the *tout ensemble* was suggestive of genius, discipline and backbone. * * * They have demonstrated that there is no such word as fail for those who are determined to succeed. It was a proud privilege to stand on that animated field yesterday, and say, ' These are American Generals and American troops, whose deeds are about to be enrolled on the scroll of immortal fame, and America is my country.' The traitor to our flag even, must have rejoiced that his pseudo-friends had been overcome by men who have shown such bravery in arms, and such mercy and moderation in victory."

Sept. 20th, Capt. Tice having resigned, Capt. Bering resumed command of the Regiment. With Capt. Tice we sent our old, tattered battle-flag to Columbus, Ohio, to be placed in the flag-room at the State House. After he arrived in Cincinnati he put it on exhibition in Wiswell's show-window on Fourth street, but it has never been seen or heard of since.

CHAPTER XIII.

Ordered to Western Louisiana — Berwick City — Teche Country — Franklin — Orange Groves — Election for Governor of Ohio — Guarding Steamers on the Teche — Surprise of the First Brigade — New Iberia — Foraging — Protection Papers.

OUR pleasant times were fast drawing to a close. Oct. 1st, we received two months' pay and were ordered on a campaign in Western Louisiana. On the 3d we embarked on the steamer "North America" and landed at Algiers, opposite New Orleans, where we took a night-train for Brashear City, a distance of eighty miles, at which place we arrived the following morning. We crossed the bay on a ferry boat and camped at Berwick City. On the 7th, the brigade advanced up through the Teche country, passing through Franklin, and camped near New Iberia, on the 9th, when our Regiment, with the 19th Ky., 77th Ills. and Chicago Mercantile Battery, were ordered back to Franklin, to garrison the place. We arrived there the 11th, and camped in the suburbs, Col. Landrum, with his staff, being camped near by, on the banks of the Teche. Co. A, in command of Capt. Cyrus Hussey, were detailed as provost-guards, and were quartered in the town.

We were now stationed in the garden-spot of Louisiana, and Franklin was one of its prettiest towns. Of this region, Longfellow, in his poem, "Evangeline," says :

"On the banks of the Teche are the towns of St. Mauer and St. Martin.
There the long-wandering bride shall be given to the bridegroom,
There the long-absent pastor regain his flock and his sheepfold.
Beautiful is the land, with its prairies and forests of fruit trees.
Under the feet a garden of flowers, and the bluest of heavens
Bending above, and resting its dome on the walls of the forest.
They who dwell there have named it the Eden of Louisiana.

  *   *   *   *   *   *   *   *   *

All the year round the orange-groves are in blossom ; and grass grows
More in a single night than in a whole Canadian summer."

It was early fall, and the weather delightful. No one who ever saw such an autumn could ever forget it. The dreamy atmosphere, drooping in the mellow haze of the mild Indian summer, almost made this lovely region a fairy land. The white cabins of the slaves were in long rows, like villages. Near by stood the elegant mansions of the wealthy planters, with broad verandas encircling the entire building. The orange groves, with their tropical fruit, were in the height of their perfection, of which a prominent writer gives the following description: "It is a beautiful sight to wander through these natural groves, watching the beautiful globes of gold peeping on all sides from the bright green foliage, bending low the branches with their weight, and exhaling a fragrance at once delicious and powerful. The fruit clings with a great deal of tenacity for a long time after it has ripened ; but during the winter and early spring it mostly falls, though the new blossoms, with their charming fragrance and pure whiteness, and young oranges, may be seen while the fruit still remains."

But the marching and counter-marching of the contending armies were leaving their marks behind. The old plantations, with their stately mansions, were going to decay ; fences, gates and ornaments of all kinds were fast disappearing ; but such is war.

Oct. 13th, the election for Governor of Ohio took place in the Regiment. Gov. Brough received 241 votes, and Vallandigham 28. Those that were absent on picket and fatigue duty did not get to vote.

While stationed at Franklin very strict discipline was enforced, and no foraging whatever was allowed, but nevertheless some members of the Regiment would venture beyond the picket-lines and gather up what poultry and other provisions they could find, and bring them into camp before daylight.

Our principal duty while stationed here, was to furnish guards for the steamboats that took the supplies up Bayou Teche to the army, encamped at New Iberia. The duty was of a very pleasant nature, more especially as the enemy did not molest us.

Oct. 23d, Lieut. Col. Lindsey arrived and took

command of the Regiment. The first brigade of our Division, while encamped in advance of the main army at New Iberia, was surprised Nov. 3d by the enemy, just as the paymaster was paying the troops. Nearly half of the brigade was captured. The paymaster, with his funds, barely escaped by timely flight in an ambulance, driven by Jonathan Pratt, of the Pioneer Corps.

On account of this surprise, the false alarms were numerous, which compelled us to be in line of battle at 4 o'clock every morning.

Nov. 11th, we were ordered to New Iberia, where we arrived the following day, and camped inside of the fortifications. Although the movements of the army were very mysterious, and no one could tell where he would be the next day, yet as soon as the arms were stacked, the Regiment went to work building quarters, as if they were going to remain there permanently. Cabins were erected out of old boards gathered up, fire-places built, bunks and bedsteads constructed, streets were laid out in regular order, which was repeated at every camp, excepting when on the march. When the cabins were completed, the next thing in order was to explore every wood, field and ravine, and in a single day the soldiers familiarized themselves with the surrounding country.

Nov. 25th, Capt. Bering, in command of 50 men of the Regiment, took charge of 240 teams, and proceeded 8 miles southwest of New Iberia, to procure forage for the army. The prairie was dotted with rich plantations, and corn and fodder was found in abundance. After the pickets were posted, to guard against a surprise, the teams were loaded; after which they returned to camp, arriving there late that evening. The planters tried in every possible way to get exempted from furnishing supplies to our army. They would exhibit what they termed "Protection Papers," claiming to be foreigners. Among the killed at the battle of Grand Coteau, a short time previous, a number were found with these papers in their pockets, which gave rise to the song, founded on that battle, commencing:

> " 'Twas on the morn of November third,
> The rebels thought they'd cage the bird,
> * * * * * *
> With 'Protection Papers' in their pocket,
> They pounced upon us like a rocket."

And the general verdict was then, that "Protection Papers" had "played out," for they were generally obtained for the purpose of taking advantage of our army.

Dec. 6th, Lieut. Col. Lindsey and ten sergeants started for Ohio, to obtain recruits, which left the Regiment again in command of Capt. Bering.

CHAPTER XIV.

Ordered to New Orleans — Embarking for Texas — Trip Across the Gulf — De Crow's Point — Dog-Tents — Distributing the Amnesty Proclamation — Planting the Flag in Texas — Skirmish Drill — Fishing and Gathering Shells — Short Rations — Cold New Year — Veterans — Ordered on Board a Condemned Vessel — Return to New Orleans — Re-enlisting — Veteran Medals — Promotions.

DECEMBER 7th, we received orders to proceed to New Orleans. We left that day and arrived at Berwick the 10th, crossed the Bay at 2 A. M. the next day, and reached Algiers by rail at noon. Here we learned that our Division was on its way to Texas by way of the Gulf.

On the 13th, the 48th, with the 130th Illinois, embarked on the steamer "Continental" for Matagorda Bay, Texas. The passage down the river from New Orleans to the Gulf was delightful. On either side could be seen broad plantations, with their elegant residences, surrounded by orange groves, the homes of the wealthy planters. The weather was delightful. The sun was shining from a clear sky, and the only breeze was a gentle wind from the Gulf, which made the voyage a very pleasant one until we reached the Gulf at 5 P. M.

Both Regiments were on deck, enjoying a ride

on the "ocean wave," when suddenly the bottom seemed to have dropped out of the Gulf. The waves ran high, and in less than an hour the majority of the men had gone below, feeling *very unwell!* During the night, the groans of the sea-sick could be heard, interspersed with a comic speech or song, from those whom the voyage had not affected. The next day it turned cold, and we encountered quite a storm. By this time the band of singers had decreased very rapidly and sea-sickness had increased correspondingly.

On the 15th, after a stormy passage, the ship was nearly blown on shore off Matagorda Bay. The ship cast anchor, which broke during the night, and we were at the mercy of the waves, until the ship was again anchored.

Our vessel being too large to cross the bar at the mouth of the bay, we were compelled to wait for a calm in order to reship on a smaller vessel, which did not occur until the evening of the 17th, when we were transferred to the steamer St. Mary's. Crossing the bar the next morning, we disembarked on De Crow's Point, Texas, which is the headland of the peninsula, situated between Matagorda Bay and the Gulf of Mexico. It is from a fourth of a mile to a mile in width, and about fifty miles long. Being elevated only a few feet above the level of the Gulf, it is completely submerged during high water, which frequently occurs during a severe storm. A few years after the war, during one of these storms, the Peninsula was thus submerged and all on it perished in the Gulf.

The peninsula is almost a barren sand-bar, but little vegetation of any kind, except wild grass, rushes and a few cactus, which grow to a very large size. Along the beach next to the Gulf, large hills or reefs of sand are formed by the wind and tide. Although we were almost surrounded by salt-water, we obtained excellent fresh drinking water by digging holes two or three feet deep in the sand.

Shortly after landing, we had our first trial of our new shelter-tents, consisting of a small strip of canvas, about four feet wide and seven long, better known as dog-tents. They were scarcely large enough for one person. They took the place of the Sibley and Bell tents, which were turned over to the Quartermaster.

President Lincoln issued a proclamation on the 8th of December, 1863, in which he offered to the Southern people one more opportunity to lay down their arms. In the proclamation, amnesty and restoration of their property (excepting slaves) were offered to all persons, excepting officers above the rank of Colonel, all civil officers of the Confederate States, and officers of the United States at the beginning of the war, who had entered the Confederate service. Raids were made in January, 1864, by the troops on the coast of Texas, in which this proclamation was scattered along the route, but if any Texans accepted the amnesty in

that part of the State, we never heard of it.
In August, 1863, Gen. Banks received instructions from Washington to plant the flag at some point in Texas without delay, in order to prevent foreign complications. A naval expedition was sent to Sabine Pass, in September, with part of the 19th Corps, under Gen. Franklin, but the navy failed to reduce the fort, and lost several vessels in the attempt. Gen. Banks then attempted to reach Texas by land, by way of New Iberia and Opelousas. (Our Division took part in the campaign, but did not get farther than New Iberia.) But he found the bayous lower than they had been for fifty years, and the country nearly destitute of supplies. The expedition was abandoned, and a descent was made under Gen. Banks, in person, on the coast of Texas, at Matagorda Bay, and at the mouth of the Rio Grande. Our Division was then sent to DeCrow's Point, Texas. This will explain the complicated movements of the army during the fall and winter of 1864, in the Department of the Gulf.

The army mule, that had stood by us in all the vicissitudes of the war, and who was always cheerful, even amid disaster and defeat, whether on half-rations or no rations at all, was, when landed at DeCrow's Point, after his ocean voyage, a most distressed and pitiful-looking object. He was completely subjugated, but in a few days he had rallied, and his familiar voice was again heard as loud as ever. The voyage seemed to have given him a renewed appetite for the wood-work of the old army wagon.

When we first arrived, our duties were comparatively light; our time was chiefly spent in skirmish-drill by bugle signals, gathering shells, bathing and fishing, with seines borrowed from the navy. In addition to the excellent fish caught, it was rare sport for the Regiment to haul out the mysterious-looking animals from the briny deep. From some unexplained cause, after our arrival we ran out of rations, but fortunately the peninsula was well stocked with sheep, which we butchered, and lived for eight or ten days almost entirely on mutton.

During cold or rainy weather, and on occasions of extra fatigue, or guard duty, the soldiers were generally supplied by the commissary department with regular rations (one gill) of whisky, but by some oversight, or "forethought," more whisky had reached us than hard-tack, which was the only time during our service, in which the Quartermaster drew more whisky than crackers; but, thanks to "kind-hearted" army contractors, it was diluted to such an extent that it was entirely harmless as a beverage.

January 1st, 1864, was the coldest day since leaving Arkansas Post, the ice freezing one inch thick in our tents, and covering the beach with the frozen spray. A soldier was brought in from the picket-line in an unconscious condition, from the effects of the Norther. During the day, the Regiment unloaded a schooner at the landing, and suffered severely from the terrific gale, that swept over the bay and dashed the waves at times over the vessel. In the North this day was known as "the cold New Year."

In the latter part of the month, Adjutant R. A. South resigned, and Lieut. Montgomery was detailed to take his place. The Government had offered a bounty of $400 to all who had served over two years, if they would enlist for another term of three years, and in addition they were to receive a furlough for thirty days, and the Regiment be entitled to the name of "Veterans." In the latter part of January an effort was made to re-enlist the Regiment, and it would have been successful had the Commanding General consented to give us our thirty days furlough immediately; but this he refused to do. Nevertheless, quite a number re-enlisted.

Lieut. Col. Parker obtained a leave of absence during the siege of Vicksburg, which was construed by Gen. Grant, in an order to Col. Sullivan, as his resignation. This order was forwarded to Columbus, Ohio. Capt. J. W. Lindsey, who was at home on furlough at the time, was promoted to the vacancy. In the meantime, Col. Parker obtained from Gen. Grant a revocation of the order accepting his resignation, stating that it was issued by mistake. He rejoined the Regiment at De Crow's Point, and was placed in command of the brigade. Shortly afterwards, he received his dismissal from the service on a charge of absence without leave.

He obtained a recommendation from the Regiment to be reinstated, and proceeded to Washington, D. C., where he had the order of his dismissal revoked, and obtained a special order to be mustered as Colonel of the Regiment. He rejoined the army after the battle of Sabine Cross-Roads.

February 1st, orders were issued for brigade-drill at 2 o'clock P. M. every day, and "grand review" twice a week. Military maneuvers in that deep, fine sand, were very fatiguing, and were not relished by the troops. To add still more to the discomfort, an order came to our Regiment, that had always worn caps, to dispense with them, and appear on drill and "grand review" with the tall regulation hats. The men growled, and General "Red Tape" came in for a good share of abuse.

Feb. 22d, we were ordered on board the steamer "Albany," a small vessel that was built for the New Jersey coast-trade, but before embarking we were informed that she was unseaworthy and would probably founder in the first gale. After this became known, the Regiment refused to embark. When Gen. Ransom, who commanded the detachment of the 13th Army Corps, heard of our refusal, he sent for the commander of the Regiment and demanded the author of the report. Upon being informed that Maj. M. C. Garber, A. Q. M., was responsible for the report, he sent for that officer and gave him a severe reprimand, and ordered Capt. Bering to take the Regiment on board without delay. There being no remedy but disobedience of orders, we embarked that evening. Our fears were well grounded, for since the war the writer met Maj. Garber, and referring to that report, he remarked that it was his duty to examine each vessel. When he inspected the "Albany" he condemned her as being unsafe for the transportation of troops, and had we encountered a storm the vessel would never have reached port.

On our trip to De Crow's Point, in December, the weather was cold and stormy, and sea-sickness so universal that we did not enjoy the voyage to a very great extent, but on our return trip the weather was mild and warm. The sun rose and set during the entire voyage in a cloudless sky, and the beauty of a "sunset at sea" was very much enjoyed by the Regiment, who lay all day on the deck, enjoying the balmy atmosphere of the Gulf. The endless variety of the finny tribe, sparkling in the waves and following in the wake of the ship, was a never-ceasing object of interest. Two species of sea-birds, the stormy petrel, which runs along the surface of the waves with great rapidity, and the sea-gull, a large, white bird, hovered around our vessel until we arrived in sight of land.

Early on the morning of the 24th, we crossed the bar and entered the Mississippi river, arriving at New Orleans that night, and disembarked the next morning at Algiers. On arrival, we had an opportunity to cross over the river to New Orleans, to lay in such supplies as we were in need of. The unusual military preparations then going on in that city, foreshadowed what soon followed —the Red River expedition. The colored brigade, composed of former slaves, made quite a formidable appearance in drill, as well as discipline, as they marched through the streets to the landing to join the expedition, and was in great contrast to the signs of "Slave Depot—Slaves Bought and Sold," that were still to be seen on the buildings where the daily auctions of the chattels were formerly held. We took the afternoon train the same day for Brashear City, where we arrived in the evening.

The plantations along the line of the railroad were far advanced in their spring work, and some of the crops were already well under cultivation.

The next morning, the 26th, we crossed the bay, which is three miles wide at that place, and camped on the west shore at Berwick City, which was rather a high-sounding title for a few empty houses and an old cotton shed. Nature had placed natural barriers against Berwick becoming a city more than in name. To the south were the Gulf marshes, and on the west an impenetrable, gloomy cypress swamp, into which the sun never penetrated, intersected by sluggish bayous and mud sloughs. It was the paradise of alligators and venomous reptiles, that grow to enormous size in that pestilence-breeding atmosphere.

Lieut. Col. Lindsey, and the ten sergeants who left for Ohio in December, rejoined the Regiment at Algiers, on its return from Texas. The Colonel brought the following commissions from Gov. Brough, for members of the Regiment : Capt. John A. Bering, promoted to Major ; Lieutenants J. R. Lynch, Geo. W. Mosgrove, C. P. Bratt, A. M. Cochran, Thomas Montgomery and R. A. South, promoted to Captains, (the latter had resigned) ; and W. J. Srofe, H. W. Day, J. K. Reed, J. M. Kendall, Joseph Stretch and C. Burkhart, promoted to First Lieutenants.

Col. Lindsey found it very difficult to obtain recruits for our Regiment while at home, for several reasons. One was that before he reached Ohio, the Regiment 1 'd been sent to Texas, which would require a ourney of over two thousand miles* to reach us, another was the hot, sickly climate and dread of the yel'ow fever. While other regiments, stationed in Tennessee and Virginia, were in a healthier climate and not so far away, therefore the new levies wisely—and for which they were not to blame—selected regiments stationed nearer home.

The time to re-enlist as veterans would expire with the last of the month, but the Regiment still refused to re-enlist in a body, unless they could get the thirty days furlough immediately after re-enlisting. Our Commanding General refused to comply with this request, until nearly the last moment, when Gen. McClernand, who had again as-

*From Cincinnati to New Orleans by steamboat 1,550 miles. From New Orleans to DeCrow's Point by ocean steamer 550 miles.

sumed command of the Thirteenth Army Corps, with headquarters at New Orleans, gave the desired promise to Lieut. Col. Lindsey. In a few days nearly the whole Regiment re-enlisted, and were sworn in for another term of three years on the 29th of February, 1864.

March 1st, Lieut. C. Burkhart was appointed Adjutant, and Sergt. W. A. Pratt promoted to Sergeant-Major. On the 3d, Capt. Cyrus Hussey, of Company A, in charge of ten sergeants, left for Columbus, Ohio, to obtain recruits for the Regiment from the drafted men. The Captain and one of the Sergeants, Harvey Cashatt, soon after their arrival at Columbus, were detailed in the Provost Marshal's office, where they remained until mustered out of the Regiment.

The following is an extract from the report of the Adjutant General of Ohio, (Gen. Cowan) for 1864:

"General Orders Nos. 191 and 305, series of 1863, from the War Department, provided for the re-enlistment of soldiers then in the service, having less than one year to serve; such re-enlisted men to be known as 'Veteran Volunteers.' The offer of large bounties and a furlough of thirty days may have facilitated these enlistments; but the stern determination on the part of the brave men who had been for more than two years battling for the cause of their country, not to lay down their arms until the enemy was subjugated, was the greatest incentive to re-enlist. They had undertaken the task of conquering the rebellion, and were unwilling to lay down their arms while an armed enemy was in their front. Large bounties are no compensation for the untold hardships, privations and dangers of a soldier's life, and no considerations of personal aggrandizement could have induced the noble sacrifices they made; nothing but the highest feeling of patriotism could have sustained them.

"While the non-veterans of our three years regiments have done their duty to their country, and retire from the service with the imperishable laurels of true and faithful soldiers, the veterans are entitled to a larger measure of praise, for having done more than they were expected to do, and having manifested in so practical a manner, their unwavering confidence in the final success of the Federal arms. All honor and praise, then, to this noble band, that is standing in the front as a cordon of triple steel, and closing steadily around the gigantic enemy of the Nation's life. More than twenty thousand of the soldiers of the State of Ohio re-enlisted as veterans, and are to-day fighting the battles of the Republic, or sleep in honored graves on the bloody field where they fell."

In 1866, all veterans in Ohio regiments received a medal, accompanied by the following order:

"STATE OF OHIO,
"ADJUTANT GENERAL'S OFFICE,
"COLUMBUS, June 1st, 1866.

"SIR:—This medal is presented to you in accordance with the following Joint Resolution of the General Assembly of Ohio, as a slight testimonial of the high appreciation by the State, of your devoted patriotism, in entering upon a second term of enlistment, without any hope or expectation of large bounties, and actuated only by the purest love of country.

"None are entitled to this medal excepting those who, being already in service in Ohio Regiments, re-enlisted for an additional term of three years.

"*Resolved, by the General Assembly of the State of Ohio*, That the Governor procure, or cause to be procured, for each veteran volunteer who re-enlisted from this State under General Orders No. 191, of 1863, a bronze medal, one and one-half inches in diameter, containing upon one side in bold relief, the following or some similar design, to-wit: Ohio personified, crowning one of her soldiers with laurel. Emblems—wheat sheaf; eagle perched on shield, bearing State arms. In the background, a steamer and tented field; springing from the wand which supports the liberty cap, a buckeye leaf. Clasp—a plain bar, on which shall be raised the buckeye and laurel; the swivel of the clasp in form of a monogram U. S. Upon the reverse side to be engraved the name of the recipient, with his regiment, battalion or battery, surrounded with a laurel wreath. The medal to be suspended by a piece of tri-colored silk ribbon, and in its artistic features to be equal to the 'Crimean medal.'

"Very Respectfully,
"B. R. COWAN."

CHAPTER XV.

Ordered to Franklin—Guarding Pontoon Train—Alexandria—Natchitoches—Capture of Pavy and McCune—Guarding the Wagon Train—Battle of Sabine Cross Roads—Out of Ammunition—Enemy in the Rear—Retreat Cut Off—Capture—On Our Way to Prison—Extracts from Gen. Ransom's Official Report—Number Captured—Extracts from Report of Committee on Conduct of the War—The Rebel General Taylor's Report of the Battle — First Night as Prisoners — Confederate Rations—School House—Marshall—Flag Song.

AS soon as the Regiment had been sworn in as veterans, letters were immediately dispatched home, to prepare for our reception on the promised furlough. But we were badly disappointed. Instead of receiving our furlough, we were ordered to Franklin, where the troops of the Gulf Department were concentrating for an expedition up Red river, at which point we arrived on the 8th.

Here the troops were organized for the campaign. The second brigade was composed of the 19th Ky., 96th, 83d and 48th Ohio, commanded by Col. Vance, of the 196th Ohio. Our Division was composed of two brigades, (1st and 2d) and under command of Col. W. J. Landrum.

March 10th, in accordance with orders issued by Gen. McClernand, the following battles were ordered to be inscribed on the colors of the 48th

Ohio Vet. Vol. Inf.: "Battle of Shiloh, Siege of Corinth, Chickasaw Bluffs, Arkansas Post, Port Gibson, Champion Hills, Black River Bridge, Siege of Vicksburg and Jackson."

We remained at Franklin until the 14th, when the Regiment took charge of the pontoon train and left for Alexandria, distant 170 miles, via Opelousas and Washington. We had a very pleasant trip, making the journey by easy marches, through the richest sugar and cotton plantations of Louisiana. As we were independent of any command, it is needless to add that the bill of fare each day contained delicacies that were not received through the commissary department.

After fourteen days' marching, we reached Alexandria on the 27th. The same evening, Col. Lindsey and Maj. Bering called on Gen. Franklin, to request him to fulfill the promise to furlough the veterans. He gave a short answer, to the effect that he could not spare a single man at that time, to say nothing of a whole veteran regiment like ours. This was poor comfort for the Regiment, and it is unnecessary to add that many used language that is called profane. Others again were like the Quaker—feared they "could not do the subject justice." Quite a number were still hopeful, and thought that as the promise was made in good faith, the furlough might arrive at any moment. But all were doomed to disappointment, for late that night, orders were received to be ready to march toward Shreveport the next morning.

During the night it rained incessantly, and toward morning it came down in torrents. At daybreak our Regiment was ordered to fall in immediately, and take the advance of the army, instead of a furlough home. This news was not very well received, for the main army had been in camp two days, resting, while our Regiment had only arrived the previous day. But swearing was no help for us, so we loaded up in the rain, many without breakfast, and with much grumbling by everybody, we took the advance.

Occasionally, on the march, some wag would call out, "Here's your veterans, going to Shreveport, on a thirty days' furlough!" A long furlough it proved, most assuredly, to the most of us. After marching a few days, the disappointment wore off, and we became somewhat reconciled. On the 2d of April, we arrived at Natchitoches, La., 127 miles above Alexandria. During our stay here, one of the soldiers of the 24th Iowa was killed in sight of camp by the rebels. He, with two of our Regiment, Pavy and McCune, of Company D, were just outside the lines, foraging, when they were surprised in a barn by two armed rebels and captured. Being unarmed, they made no resistance. After tying them loosely together, they were marched back some distance and seated on a log, when the rebels decided to shoot them, and began tying them more securely. The Iowa soldier, who was in the middle, attempted to release himself; whereupon one of their captors fired, killing him instantly. At this Pavy broke loose and ran for camp, with one of his captors after him, while McCune was knocked down with a musket by the other, who then turned and watched the race. McCune, in the meantime, recovering, untied himself from his dead comrade, and made good his escape, as did also Pavy, who came into camp almost exhausted. A force of cavalry was sent out and the body of the dead soldier was brought in, and the house and barn burnt. The two rebels were afterward captured, but claimed they were Confederate soldiers, at home on a furlough. The rebels threatened retaliation if they were executed, so they were afterwards exchanged.

From the day we started on the Red River expedition, we were like the Israelites of old, accompanied by a cloud (of smoke) by day, and a pillar of fire by night. The rebels had a company of cavalry setting fire to all the cotton along our route. From the cotton the flames would spread to the cotton-sheds and out-houses, and frequently reached the dwellings of the planters and cabins of the slaves. This was one of the curious phases of the war—to see the rebels bent on the destruction of their own property.

We left Natchitoches April 6th, for Shreveport, La., by way of Pleasant Hill and Mansfield. We guarded the train on the 7th, and did not get into camp until the drums were beating the last tattoo. The Regiment stacked arms, and while peparing our late supper, we sat aronnd the cheerful camp fires, discussing the campaign, which as usual drifted into reminiscences of the peaceful days before the war, and ended with the query, when shall we get our long promised furlough? little dreaming what was in store for us on the coming morrow. We started next morning, April 8th, with the brigade, at 5½ o'clock. The enemy, who had been easily driven the day before by the cavalry, became quite stubborn, and it at times required the aid of the infantry to dislodge them. We marched until half past ten, when we arrived at St. Patrick's Bayou, which Gen. Franklin selected as our camping-ground.

We had scarcely stacked arms, when Gen. Ransom ordered one brigade forward on double-quick. We found great difficulty in passing the cavalry train, which obstructed the entire road through the dense pine forest. At intervals we could hear the heavy firing in our front, indicating that there was work ahead for us. Soon we began to see the wounded and dead, along the road, which showed clearly that the rebels were fighting at every point. We had nearly reached the Sabine Cross-Roads, when Col. Lindsey ordered Maj. Bering to take command of the Regiment, he being ordered to take command of the brigade by Col. Vance, who was sick. The Colonel did not leave the field, but partially recovering, he remained during the battle. He retained Lieut. Col. Lindsey to assist him, and was killed during the engagement.

We arrived at the front between one and two o'clock P. M. In our front was a cleared field, and on the opposite side was a belt of timber, where our cavalry was skirmishing with the enemy. Col. Landrum ordered our brigade across to the right of the road, on double-quick, to take position in the edge of the woods. We charged across the open field and over a small stream, then up to the timber. Here the men threw off their knapsacks, advanced a short distance and halted.

We remained in line of battle until near 4 o'clock, when the cavalry pickets came back on a gallop through our lines, saying the enemy was advancing in strong force. We occupied a narrow strip of timber, and the rebels an open field beyond. Midway between the two armies was a rail fence, running parallel with our line of battle, at the further edge of the timber. We were ordered forward, and had proceeded but a short distance, when we discovered the long line of rebel infantry, coming on double-quick, to gain the fence. It now became an exciting race, but fortunately we reached the fence while the enemy was still about fifty yards distant. . Our men, dropping on their knees, rested their rifles on the fence and delivered a volley with terrible effect. The enemy delivered their fire entirely too high, but stood their ground for half an hour, when the whole line wavered in our front and retreated in disorder, leaving the ground covered with killed and wounded. Cheer after cheer went up from our troops when they saw the rebels flying from the field.

In a short time, however, they reformed, and came up in two lines, and renewed the attack, but were repulsed as before. Their field-officers being mounted, were picked off as fast as they came in range. The Division held its position for nearly two hours, against the combined forces of the rebel Generals, Dick Taylor, Walker and Mouton, when suddenly the right of the Regiment was forced back from the fence, caused by an enfilading fire from the enemy. The 19th Kentucky, who occupied the position on our right, had received orders from Col. Landrum to retreat, but waiting for our Regiment, which for some cause had not received the order, they changed front to our rear, and remained with us.

The brigade was now ordered by its commander, (Lieut.-Col. Lindsey) to fall back gradually. We left the fence and retreated about fifty yards, where we attempted to make another stand under a heavy fire, but we were entirely out of ammunition and our supply cut off, which made our condition very critical. They soon closed in and demanded our surrender. With no other alternative, the Regiment reluctantly threw down their arms and empty cartridge-boxes, and were hurried to the rear, while our batteries from the third Division, which had just arrived, began throwing shell and solid shot into our midst. We passed over the battle-field, that was strewn with rebel dead and wounded, and met line after line of rebel infantry and artillery, who were hurrying forward toward the scene of action. We began to think their numbers had been under-estimated, and were fearful of the consequences, but they were groundless, for on the following day (the 9th) the rebel army was defeated by our forces at Pleasant Hill.

During the engagement several details were sent to the rear to bring up a supply of ammunition, but they were cut off, captured or killed. Among the latter was Adjutant C. Burkhart. The following is a list of the killed and wounded, as near as we could ascertain:

Lieut. Col. Lindsey, wounded in arm; Adjutant C. Burkhart, killed; Capt. G. W. Mosgrove, of Co. D, wounded in thigh, and the only officer that escaped capture; Capt. A. M. Cochran, of Co. E, wounded in foot; Co. B, Amos Fuller and Wm. Fuller, wounded; Co. C, Samuel Hair, mortally wounded through the breast; he was taken prisoner and died a few days after; Morgan Tedrick, wounded slightly; Co. E, Carl Huff, wounded; Co. G, Wm. Barron, killed, G. Bohan, wounded; Co. H, Wm. Cast, killed, Jos. Quinn, Wm. Riley, Jos. Dorly, Pat. Conner, Wm. Bamgrove and Charles Keener, wounded; and the following officers captured: Lieut.-Col. J. W. Lindsey, Maj. J. A. Bering, Captains James Sowry, A. M. Cochran, Daniel Gunsaullus and Thomas Montgomery, Lieutenants W. J. Srofe, H. W. Day and

M. McCaffrey. Total 9, and 168 enlisted men. Col. Lindsey was sent to the hospital, and at the close of the campaign was exchanged, with the rest of the wounded that fell into the hands of the enemy during the Red River expedition.

The Regiment fought with the skill and bravery of veterans, showing that they had been well drilled in the art of fighting, and had profited by the experience gained on former battle-fields, as was proved by the large number of killed and wounded among the rebels who undertook to drive us from the fence. Such coolness is seldom witnessed on the battle-field, and we could record many daring deeds performed by individuals during the engagement, but where all behaved so coolly what is said in praise of one will apply to all. Nevertheless, after completely defeating the enemy in our front, to be overpowered when out of ammunition, by a superior force in our rear, when we had a large army lying in camp six or seven miles back, was a poor reward for such heroism; but such are the fortunes of war.

Gen. T. E. G. Ransom passed through our Regiment during the engagement, cheering the men with his presence. He also testified to their bravery in his official report of the battle. To give a more general idea of the engagement, we will insert a copy of Gen. Ransom's official report. He commanded the Thirteenth Army Corps, was wounded in the leg during the engagement, and sent to New York, where this report was written:

"NEW YORK CITY, June 11, 1864.

"SIR: I have the honor to make the following report of the movements of the troops under my command, consisting of the Third Division, Thirteenth Army Corps, Brig.-Gen. R. A. Cameron, commanding, and the Fourth Division, Thirteenth Army Corps, under command of Col. W. J. Landrum, on the 6th, 7th and 8th of April, 1864.

"On the 6th of April, my detachment, having the advance of the infantry column, moved from Natchitoches at 6 o'clock A. M., in the rear of the cavalry division, and being constantly delayed by the baggage-train of the latter, went into camp late on Bayou Mayon, having marched nineteen miles on the Pleasant Hill road. Moved at half-past 5 o'clock A. M. on the 7th, the head of the column arrivng at Pleasant Hill, 19 miles, at 2 o'clock P. M., overtaking the cavalry train on the road, and Dudley's brigade of cavalry at Pleasant Hill. When these had moved from our camping-grounds, I went into camp about 4 o'clock P. M., though my train and rear-guard did not arrive till late at night. At 10 o'clock P. M., I received an order to send a brigade to Gen. Lee, commanding the cavalry division, at or before 5 o'clock the following morning. In compliance with the above order, Col. Landrum moved with the first brigade of his division, and reported to Gen. Lee at daylight on the 8th.

"Under orders from Maj.-Gen. Franklin, I moved the remainder of the Corps forward at half-past 5 o'clock A. M., and arrived with the advance at St. Patrick's Bayou, at half-past 10 o'clock A. M., our march having as before been retarded by the cavalry train. Gen. Franklin had previously designated this creek as my camping-ground, and I accordingly ordered the Third Division, and the second brigade of the Fourth Division, into camp at half-past 10 A. M. Before the order had been complied with, a request was received from Gen. Lee, asking for more infantry, to relieve that already with him, and Gen. Franklin directed me to send the second brigade of the Fourth Division, Col. J. W. Vance commanding, to relieve the first brigade, who were reported as worn out with hard skirmishing and marching.

"The second brigade moved forward at 11 A. M. and at my request, Gen. Franklin authorized me to go to the front, and see that the first brigade was relieved by the second. I immediately went forward, and on the road received a dispatch, of which the following is a copy :

"'12, noon. Gen. Ransom : My men have skirmished and marched through the bushes and thickets for 8 or 9 miles. They have no water, and are literally worn out. Can you have them relieved soon ? Gen. Lee insists on our pushing forward. " 'W. J. LANDRUM,
" 'Col. Com'd'g 4th Div.'

"The infantry finding much difficulty in passing the cavalry train, which obstructed the road, I went on in advance of them, and arrived at the front, 5½ miles from St. Patrick's Bayou, about half-past 1 o'clock P. M. I found that our forces had just driven the enemy across an open field, and were shelling him from a fine position on a ridge, which Col. Landrum occupied with his infantry and Nim's battery, about 2 o'clock P. M. It was determined to halt here, in order to allow the second brigade to come up and relieve the first.

"In company with Brig.-Gen. Stone and Lieut. Higby, signal-officer, I went to the front line of skirmishers, and carefully reconnoitered the position of the enemy. We were able to perceive two batteries, and a large force of infantry in line of battle, in the edge of the woods, from a half to three-quarters of a mile from our front, and also considerable bodies of infantry moving down the road leading to our right and rear.

"Hearing of the arrival of Maj.-Gen. Banks and staff upon the field, about 3 o'clock P. M., I reported to him, and advised him of the position and apparent strength of the enemy, and from him received instructions as to the disposition of my troops on the field, and of those momentarily expected. Upon the arrival of the brigade, the positions of two of its regiments—the 83d and 96th —were assigned by Maj. Leiber, of Gen. Banks' staff, on the opposite flank from that determined on by Gen. Banks and myself, and in a position where I should not have placed them.

"The infantry on the right of the road occupied a narrow belt of timber, dividing two large plantations, and having open, though broken, ground in front, and in the rear a cultivated field, which descended to a small creek, and thence rose to the timber, one-half mile to the rear of our line.

"Nim's battery was posted on a hill, near the road, about two hundred yards to the left of the belt of timber, and was supported by the 23d Wisconsin infantry, which was on the left and behind the crest of the hill, with open fields in front. The 67th Indiana supported the battery on the right, joined by the 77th and 130th Illinois, 48th Ohio, 19th Kentucky, 96th Ohio, a section of mounted artillery, and the 83d Ohio, making in all 2,413 infantry. The cavalry and mounted infantry under Gen. Lee, were posted on the flanks and rear, having Col. Dudley's brigade on the left and Col. Lucas's on the right, and also skirmishers deployed in front of the infantry.

"The skirmishing continued throughout the afternoon, becoming sharp on the right about half-past 2 o'clock P. M. At this time Col. Lucas reported that his skirmishers on the extreme right were driven in, and that a few of his men on that flank had been captured. About 4 o'clock P. M. the enemy commenced advancing his lines across the open fields in our front, and east of the road. I directed Col. Landrum to advance our right, consisting of the 83d, 96th and 48th Ohio, 130th Illinois, and 19th Kentucky, and he immediately opened fire on the enemy, now in good range, and advancing in two lines. We drove back his first line in confusion upon his second, but recovering, he again advanced till, unable to endure our heavy fire, he halted about two hundred yards from our front, where many of his men lay down and returned our fire. I felt confident that this portion of our line could not be broken, but while moving toward the left flank I was informed that the enemy were pressing us at that point, and that the mounted infantry were falling back.

"At this time Captain White, chief of artillery, reported that the Chicago Mercantile Battery, Lieut. Cone commanding, and the First Indiana Battery, Capt. Klaus commanding, had arrived, and I directed him to place them in an advantageous position on a ridge to the east of the road, and near a house occupied as Gen. Banks' headquarters, where they opened on the enemy, who had shown himself in strong force on the left. * *

"Our left flank was completely turned, and the enemy, having taken Nim's battery, were in strong force on the hill, and pouring a destructive fire into the batteries of the Fourth Division. I ordered the latter to the rear, to a point on the right of the road, and sent Capt. Dickey, my Ass't. Adj't.-General, to order Col. Landrum to withdraw his Division to the edge of the timber in our rear. Capt. Dickey was to send aides to the different regiments, to give the orders direct, in case he should not find Col. Landrum, but while in performance of this duty, this gallant officer fell senseless from his horse, mortally wounded. Owing to the loss of Capt. Dickey before he had communicated my orders, some of the regiments did not receive them until they were surrounded and their retreat cut off, while they were gallantly fighting a superior force in their front.

"In company with Col. Landrum, I was, as the troops arrived, re-forming the line in the edge of the woods, when I was severely wounded in the knee and was carried to the rear. I found the woods and roads full of mounted men, flying in confusion from the field.

"I desire here to bear witness to the gallantry of Brig.-Gen. Stone, who was on the left of the line with Gen. Lee. He used the small force of infantry to the best advantage, in bravely but unsuccessfully endeavoring to repulse the overwhelming force of the enemy. Col. Landrum, commanding Fourth Division, was conspicuous, and everywhere present, encouraging all by his own gallant conduct, and judicious disposition of his men. * * *

"I was an eye-witness of the bravery and soldierly bearing of Lieut.-Col. Cowan and Maj. Mann, of the 19th Kentucky, Lieut. Col. Baldwin, 83d Ohio, Maj. Bering, 48th Ohio, Maj. Reed, 130th Illinois, and know the gallantry with which their men repulsed the enemy in his first attack. * * * * * * * * *

"The conduct of the troops under my command was all that I could ask. They repulsed a superior force in their front, and but for the movement of a large body of the enemy upon our left, which could not be prevented with the force at our command, would have held the first line, and, with the assistance of Gen. Cameron's Third Division, could have checked the enemy till the arrival of the Nineteenth Corps. * * * * *

"I have the honor to be, Major, very respectfully, your obedient servant,

"T. E. G. RANSOM,* Brig.-Gen. Vols.
"Maj. Wickham Hoffman, Ass't. Adju't.-Gen."

After the Fourth Division was captured, the Third Division of the Thirteenth Army Corps arrived, were, in turn, overpowered, being compelled to fall back before superior numbers, and the enemy were not checked until they came up with the Nineteenth Corps, about two or three miles from where we had been captured.

Seven miles back from the battle-ground the Nineteenth Corps was encamped, numbering five or six thousand men, and fifteen miles back, Gen. A. J. Smith, with seven or eight thousand. The main army was in camp, out of supporting distance, to the number of thirteen or fourteen thousand men, while the battle was fought on our side with twenty-four hundred, besides the cavalry,

---
*Died of disease in the Atlanta campaign.

and we had opposed to us an army of ten thousand rebels.

In this engagement the rebels captured 1,200 prisoners, besides the wounded, 20 pieces of artillery, and 250 cavalry wagons. But it was a dear-bought victory for the enemy. The 17th Texas was badly cut up, and the Crescent regiment, composed of young men of the first families of New Orleans, was almost annihilated. It lost every field officer, and many of its company officers, while the 18th and 28th Louisiana suffered severely in killed and wounded, both of officers, and men, and Gen. Mouton, a favorite officer, was killed.

The following account of the battle is from the Confederate Lieutenant-General, Richard Taylor's, " Personal Experiences of the Late War ":

" Leaving Green, I returned to Mansfield, stopping on the road to select my ground for the morrow. This was in the edge of a wood, fronting an open field, eight hundred yards in width by twelve hundred in length, through the center of which the road to Pleasant Hill passed. On the opposite side of the field was a fence, separating it from the pine forest, which, open on the higher ground and filled with underwood on the lower, spread over the country. The position was three miles in front of Mansfield, and covered a cross-road leading to the Sabine. On either side of the main Mansfield-Pleasant Hill road, at two miles' distance, was a road parallel to it, and connected by this Sabine cross-road.

"My troops reached the position in front of Sabine cross-road at an early hour on the 8th, and were disposed as follows : On the right of the road to Pleasant Hill, Walker's infantry division of three brigades, with two batteries ; on the left, Mouton's, of two brigades and two batteries. As Green's men, (composed of three brigades of cavalry, under Generals Bee, Mayor and Bagby) came in, they took position, dismounted, on Mouton's left.

"A regiment of horse was posted in each of the parallel roads mentioned, and DeBray's cavalry, with McMahon's battery, held in reserve on the main road. Dense forest prevented the employment of much artillery, and, with the exception of McMahon's, which rendered excellent service, none was used in the action. I had on the field 5,300 infantry, 3,000 horse, and 500 artillerymen, in all, 8,800 men, a very full estimate, and on the morrow Churchill, with 4,400 muskets, would be up. * * *

"The enemy showing no disposition to advance, at 4 P. M. I ordered a forward movement of my whole line. The ardor of Mouton's troops, especially the Louisianians, could not be restrained by their officers. Crossing the field under a heavy fire of artillery and small arms, the division reached the fence, paused for a moment to draw breath, then rushed into the wood on the enemy.

Here our loss was severe. Gen. Mouton was killed, as were Colonels Armand, Beard and Walker, commanding the 18th, the Crescent, and 28th Louisiana regiments of Gray's brigade.* Maj. Canfield, of the Crescent, also fell, and Lieut.-Col. Clack, of the same regiment, was mortally wounded. As these officers went down, others, among whom Adjutant Blackman was conspicuous, seized the colors and led on the men. Polignac's brigade, on the left of Gray's, also suffered heavily. Col. Noble, 17th Texas, with many others, was killed. Polignac, left in command by the death of Mouton, displayed ability and pressed the shattered division steadily forward. Randall, with his fine brigade, supported him on the right; while Major's dismounted men, retarded by dense wood, much to the impatience of Gen. Green, gradually turned the enemy's right, which was forced back, with loss of prisoners and guns.

"On the right of the main road, Gen. Walker, with Waul's and Scurry's brigades, encountered but little resistance until he had crossed the open field and entered the wood. Finding that he outflanked the enemy's left, he kept his right brigade, Scurry's, advanced, and swept everything before him.

"'The first Federal line, consisting of all the mounted force and one division of the 13th Army Corps, was in full flight, leaving prisoners, guns

---

*Gen. Gray's brigade occupied the position in front of our brigade.

and wagons in our hands. Two miles in the rear of the first position, the 2d Division of the 13th Corps was brought up, but was speedily routed, losing guns and prisoners ; and our advance continued. Near sunset, four miles from our original position, the 19th Army Corps was found, drawn up on a ridge, overlooking a small stream. Fatigued and distressed by their long advance through dense wood, my men made no impression for a time on this fresh body of troops ; but possession of the water was all-important, for there was none other between this and Mansfield. Walker, Green and Polignac led on their weary men, and I rode down to the stream. There was some sharp work, but we persisted, the enemy fell back, and the stream was held just as twilight faded into darkness. * * *

"Sitting by my camp-fire, to await the movement of Churchill's column, I was saddened by the recollection of the many dead, and the *pleasure of victory was turned to grief as I counted the fearful cost at which it had been won*. Of the Louisianians fallen, most were acquaintances, many had been neighbors and friends ; and they were gone. Above all, the death of gallant Mouton affected me. * * * Our total loss in killed, wounded and missing, (during the campaign) was 3,376."

The plan of the campaign was for Gen. Steele, with a force of 10,000 men, to form a junction with Gen. Banks at or near Shreveport, but Gen. Steele, having lost a large portion of his supply train, was compelled to abandon the expedition before he got within 100 miles of Shreveport.

After our capture at Sabine Cross Roads, the enemy was held in check by the 19th Corps, and the army fell back to Pleasant Hill during the night. The following day the battle of Pleasant Hill was fought, in which the rebels were defeated and driven from the field. The following morning at daylight the army retreated to Grand Ecore, where it was delayed on account of the navy until April 22d, when the retreat was resumed and the enemy found in a strong position at Cane river; but after a severe engagement they were dislodged and the army reached Alexandria April 25th. The following day the fleet of gunboats and transports arrived at the head of the falls, but owing to the low stage of the river they could not cross them. The great danger was that the whole fleet would have to be destroyed, to keep it from falling into the hands of the enemy. At this critical period Lieut.-Col. Baily, of the 4th Wis. Vol's., made a proposition to erect a dam at the foot of the falls and two wing dams on both sides of the river above, and by this means, force the water into the main channel, of sufficient depth to allow the fleet to pass over the falls. The work was commenced April 30th, by the Pioneer Corps and large details from the army. The soldiers labored zealously day and night, in the water waist-deep, until May 13th, when the last vessel, amid the cheers of the army and navy, passed over the falls.

The army then evacuated Alexandria, and resumed its march to the Mississippi river, where, after several sharp engagements with the enemy, they reached Simmsport May 16th, and Gen. Canby relieved Gen. Banks of the command of the Department of the Gulf.

Thus ended the Red River expedition, which, under able generalship, might have struck the rebel cause in the Southwest a severe blow, but instead of that it revived to a great extent the drooping spirits of the enemy.

The immense wagon-train of the cavalry received its full share of blame for the failure of the expedition, of which a military critic says : "Gen. Banks made his great march up Red river with his wagons as his advance-guard. The scheme worked finely, and would have been a complete success if the enemy had not interfered with the arrangement."

The total loss of Gen. Banks' army during the campaign, was 289 killed, 1,541 wounded, and 2,150 missing ; total, 3,980. The enemy's loss, according to Gen. Taylor, was 3,976, our loss being over half in prisoners, while the greater portion of theirs was in killed and wounded.

From the summary of the report of the Congressional Committee, before whom the testimony was taken, we gather the following :

"The whole expedition presents many remarkable features. It was undertaken without the direction of any one, so far as the evidence shows, and the authorities at Washington did not furnish the troops which the General commanding the expedition considered necessary for the purpose. In the absence of all orders requiring this expedition to be undertaken, and after the refusal of the authorities at Washington to furnish the troops asked for, it was entered upon by the Commanding General, as shown by the evidence, against his judgment and in the belief that it must necessarily fail; and it was prosecuted at an immense sacrifice of life, of property and valuable time, after the development of facts that utterly precluded all hope of success. Its only results, in addition to the disgraceful disasters that attended it, were of a commercial and political character. The commercial transactions were conducted by speculators, who followed the army with and without permits. The political transaction was the holding of elections in the camps of the army while reorganizing a civil government in the State of Louisiana," etc. etc.

Such is the report of the Committee on the Conduct of the War, of which Senator Wade was chairman, in regard to the Red River Expedition, under Gen. Banks.

From the battle-field we were taken to Mansfield, about four miles distant, and put in the court-house yard. After taking our names, they marched us about two miles out of town, and guarded us in a field. The night was cold and chilly, and as we had no blankets, we set fire to some old logs and crowded around as closely as possible, in order to keep warm. About eleven o'clock that night we received a few crackers and some bacon.

The next day, April 9th, the prisoners, numbering 182 officers and 1,000 men, in charge of a battalion of Louisiana cavalry, started for Camp Ford, Texas. After marching 15 or 20 miles, we were corraled for the night. Here we received our first regular rations from the Confederacy, which consisted of a pint of musty corn meal, coarsely ground, and a slice of salt beef. As we had no cooking utensils, some procured boards, upon which they baked their bread, while others baked it in the ashes. A number had their rations cooked at a house near camp, for which the charge was so exorbitant that in the future they did their own cooking. If at any time we were so fortunate as to procure a pot or kettle from the guards, we would have a sumptuous feast of mush, which, for want of spoons, was eaten with paddles.

The following day we proceeded on our way to Texas. In places we found the road lined with slaves, in charge of their masters, who were hurrying them to Texas to prevent them from falling into the hands of the "Yankees." The contracted brows of the masters indicated their hatred, while the happy countenances of the slaves showed that they considered us their best friends. For the benefit of both parties, we would sing,

"Ole Massa runn'd—aha!
De darkeys stay, oho!
It must be now dat de kingdom am a comin',
An' de year ob Jubilo!"

which would make the masters frown and the darkies grin.

On the 11th we passed through Lagrange. The only building of note was a large school-house, that was used as a hospital, and was full of sick and wounded rebels. We camped that evening on one of the very few streams that are found in that part of the country, as the surface is undulating, and the soil sandy, gravelly and dry, with but few springs, or running streams. Occasionally, on the march, we would pass large crowds of men and women, waiting at some cross-road to catch a glimpse of the "Yankees." While passing, we generally sang some Union song for their benefit. At one place, quite a number of ladies had collected from the neighborhood of a small village, and we sang for them the following war-song:

"THE STARS AND THE STRIPES SHALL WAVE IN EVERY STATE,
AS WE GO MARCHING ON,"

to the tune of "John Brown," when several of them cried out "No, they shan't! No, they shan't!" accompanied with gestures that were quite amusing. We continued our song, one key higher. Soon after we were halted for a rest, at the only school-house seen outside of a town or city on our way to prison. It was occupied by a lady teacher and a few small scholars. She directed the children to give the prisoners what they had left from their dinners. She was from the State of Illinois, and the war found her teaching in Texas.

On the fourth day's march we arrived at Marshall, Texas, and camped in the woods near the city. The next morning we passed through the place. The whole surrounding population turned out to see the "Yankees" who had been captured. Some really believed that they had made prisoners of the whole army. Our boys would halloo at them and sarcastically tell them they had captured all the "Yankees," "the war was now over," etc. While passing through the main street, we came to a large crowd, who occupied the sidewalks and windows. The guards, who were principally boys, coaxed us to sing that "Flag Song," ("Rally Round the Flag, Boys.") It was no sooner said than done, and when we came to the chorus:

"Down with the traitors and up with the stars,"

one old lady ran out of the crowd, very much excited, and called to the guards to "make the Yankees quit that singing." But they enjoyed it too much to order us to stop. The old lady kept on shaking her fist at us, and stamping her feet, but whatever she said was drowned in the chorus of the "Union Forever," sung by about five hundred Yankees, who felt miserable enough to make everybody else feel so.

CHAPTER XVI.

PRISON LIFE IN TEXAS.

"In the prison cell I sit, thinking, mother dear, of you,
And our bright and happy home, so far away;
Yet the tears they fill my eyes, spite of all that I can do,
Though I try to cheer my comrades and be gay."

Arrival at Camp Ford—The Stockade—Building Huts—Col. Allen Relieved by Col. Border—Adjutant McEachan—"Keno"—Tied Up by the Thumbs—Rations Cut Off—The Famous Order, "Kill All Recaptured Prisoners"—New Recruits from Gen. Steel's Army—Building Hospital—Poisonous Insects—Fourth of July Celebration—Exchange of One Thousand Prisoners—New "Cart-el"—Tunneling—Our Flag in Prison—Different Trades—Inflation Prices—Old Citizen Dumped—Brutal Treatment of Prisoners—Escape of Maj. Bering and Lieut. Srofe—New Commander.

AFTER seven days weary marching, we arrived at Camp Ford, situated four miles east of Tyler, Smith county, Texas, an old prison, which contained about 600 Union soldiers. It was commonly called "the Stockade," and had been enlarged from about three acres to six, in order to make room for new-comers. It was surrounded by logs set into the ground, and projecting out five or six feet, on the outside of which the guards were stationed. When we came in sight of the stockade, all eyes were directed toward what was to be our future home. The sight was not very encouraging. Inside of what appeared to be a large pen, were a few log cabins scattered around, with here and there a hut, made of brush, or a hovel, made altogether of yellow clay. Every cabin, and every available high spot of ground, were covered by the old prisoners, who were dressed in "tatters and rags," and all anxious to get a glimpse of "Gen. Banks' Army," which the rebels reported as being captured. We were marched to the upper part of the stockade and drawn up in line, when Col. Allen, the prison commander, addressed the prisoners to the effect, that each regiment would be allowed the length of the ground they occupied, with a width of twenty feet, for their quarters, and told them to make themselves as comfortable as possible. We thought this rather cool, as we had no blankets or covering of any kind. We had marched 500 miles since we left Berwick Bay, March 7th, and to say we were tired, foot-sore, hungry and discouraged, would be stating it mildly.

The officers of our Regiment were kindly invited by the old officers in prison, to their several shanties, and provided with supper and lodging until they succeeded in building a residence of their own. For this kindness, the officers of the Regiment will forever consider themselves under obligations to the old prisoners. The following day the officers of the Regiment decided to build a log cabin. We borrowed one ax, and paid for the use of another, and by two weeks hard work we had succeeded in erecting a log hut, by carrying the logs half a mile. In the course of time the prisoners succeeded in building shanties, brush huts, or rude hovels, by burrowing in the ground.

One difficulty in making shelter was the scarcity of axes; still greater, to get permits to go outside. The rebel authorities claimed that they did the best they could, but this was a mistake. It would have been but very little trouble for them, with the slaves at their command, to have built log cabins sufficient to shelter every prisoner. But the enterprising and industrious Northern soldiers only asked permission to go outside and get the necessary material, which was granted to so few at a time, that very little progress could be made.

While engaged in building, the time passed rapidly, but after that was done, it began to hang heavily on our hands. The few books in camp were soon read; playing chess became irksome after a while, and too much sleeping during the day spoiled our rest at night.

Our meals did not occupy a great deal of our time. After roll-call we had breakfast, which consisted of corn bread and corn coffee, and dinner as soon thereafter as possible, consisting of corn bread and beef, our supper being made up of the scraps of the two previous meals, provided there had been anything left.

We had settled down and were getting used to the new order of things, when, about the middle of May, ten or twelve hundred prisoners that had been captured at Marks' Mills, Arkansas, from Gen. Steel's command, were turned into the stockade. A short time afterward, another party arrived, consisting of about six hundred prisoners, generally known as Col. Leek's men. They had been sent forward for exchange, but on account of some difficulty, were returned to their old quarters after an absence of eight or ten weeks. They were decidedly a hard-looking set of men, as they had been in prison for nearly a year, and during that time had not received a single article of clothing.

After eight or ten weeks under Col. Allen, as prison commander, he was superseded by Lieut.-Col. Border. Col. Allen was not a bad man at heart. He did not misuse any of the prisoners, although he never granted them any particular favors. He put off every one with fair promises, which were seldom redeemed.

Our new commander, Col. Border, was somewhat on the "black-flag" order—"Kill as you go" —but too indolent to carry out any of his threats. He had a worthy tool in the person of his Adjutant, Lieut. McEachan, who was always contriving something to cause trouble, that he might "shoot Yankees by the wholesale," as he remarked on one occasion.

We were well supplied with gamblers, and their

favorite game was called "Keno." Sometimes as many as a dozen different gambling institutions were in full blast in the public square. Every few days Adjutant McEachan, with a squad of soldiers, would slip in and surround the gamblers and capture their funds. To avoid these raids, the gamblers would place a sentinel, who, when he saw McEachan coming, would give the watch-word, "Keno," which was repeated all over the camp, and thus they were protected from future raids. But this watch-word, "Keno," McEachan thought was applied to him, for whenever he appeared he was greeted on all sides with the cry of "Keno," which so exasperated him that he would take whole squads out and punish them for refusing to point out the parties who called out "Keno." To deliver up a fellow-prisoner was never thought of for a moment; consequently, the whole squad would be punished, by tying their thumbs to a beam overhead, and compelling them to stand with their bare feet on sharp sticks driven into the ground. He finally withheld the rations from the whole camp, unless the leaders of the "Keno" cry would be delivered up for special punishment. But Col. Flora and Capt. DeHart, of the 46th Indiana, having sent word to the commander at Tyler, notifying him of the action of the Adjutant, he ordered Col. Border to supply the prisoners with rations without delay. But for the prompt action of Col. Anderson, the commander at Tyler, there is no telling how the matter might have ended. Had the Adjutant persisted in his threat to starve us into compliance with his terms, the four thousand desperate and half-starved prisoners would no doubt have overpowered the guards and flooded the country.

After the public reprimand of McEachan by Col. Anderson, he did not torment the Yankees by wholesale, but made individuals feel his power. Prisoners recaptured in the attempt to escape, were made to stand on stumps or barrels, for days, without hats or shoes, in the broiling sun, while a guard stood over them with loaded musket, to prevent them from sitting down. Others were tied up by the thumbs in the manner already described, or sent to jail at Tyler, in irons, while several guards, who had shot a number of our men without provocation, were rewarded by promotion for the deed. Then came the famous order to kill all re-captured Yankees:

"Hereafter, any Federal prisoner, being detected in trying to make his escape from the prison, either in the act or after he has made his escape, will be shot by the one capturing him. By order of LIEUT.-COL. BORDER,
"Commanding Camp Ford Prison.
" B. W. McEACHAN, Lieut. and Act'g Adj't."

In this way he kept the camp in a continual state of feverish excitement. In the meantime, additions were being made almost weekly to our number, from Gen. Banks' army, on Red River, and Gen. Steel's army, in Arkansas, until the pen was almost over-crowded. Sickness now began to increase, and the so-called hospital for the prisoners, composed of a log cabin and some brush huts, was soon filled. The sanitary condition of the stockade, and the wants of the sick, are well described in the report of the Prison Surgeon, which is as follows :

"TYLER, Texas, June 14, 1864.
"*Surgeon J. M. Hayden, Chief Med. Bureau, Trans-Miss. Dep't.* :

" SIR :—In obedience to orders, I reported to Col. Anderson, Commander of Federal prisoners, who placed me on duty as Surgeon in charge. I at once examined the sanitary condition of the stockade, and, although my mind was prepared by representation, to meet with abundant material for disease, it fell far short of the reality. The enclosed ground is entirely too small for the number of men, (over 4,500), and it would be impossible to make them healthy in such a crowded condition. The filth and offal have been deposited in the streets and between the quarters, from which arises a horrible stench. A great number of enlisted men have no quarters or shelter, and have to sleep out on the ground, with not even a blanket to cover them. Some of the sick are thus situated, and I am making preparations to provide for their wants and to make them comfortable. We have a hospital in course of erection, and will need bedding very much. The popular prejudice here is so strong against them, that I can get no facilities from the people. I am ready to receive into the hospital a few, if we had the articles, and they are not to be had here. * * * *

"Very Resp'f'y, Your Ob'dt Serv't.
"F. M. MEAGHER."

The Surgeon's report had no more effect on the "Medical Bureau," than his appeal to the "prejudiced people." The only result was, the rebels furnished an old mule and cart, to haul off the garbage.

The enlargement of the hospital to meet the wants of the sick, was done by volunteers from among the prisoners, who erected two buildings, one thirty-five by ten feet, the other about fifty feet long and twenty feet wide, a short distance from the stockade, which was soon filled with emaciated forms. Only the worst cases were allowed to enter. Even then there was not room for half—many dying in the stockade.

The physicians, stewards and nurses were all volunteers, who were stimulated by a generous spirit to assist in relieving the wants of their fellow-prisoners, by administering the meager allowance of medicines and rations of corn bread and beef, which was not very inviting to those who, from disease and exposure, were on the verge of the grave. A large spring in the southwest corner, strongly impregnated with sulphur, supplied the prisoners with wholesome water, which was a great luxury in that miserable pen.

We had to exercise great caution on account of the numerous poisonous insects in and around the prison. A soldier was bitten on the neck, which became very much swollen, but the surgeons could not do anything to relieve him, and after much suffering the man died. A short time afterward, a tarantula was found under a board in his cabin. The tarantula is in fact an overgrown spider, and sometimes attains the size of the hand. He is a repulsive looking object, with his glaring black eyes and frightful claws. His bite is said to be more fatal than that of the rattlesnake. They were to be found everywhere under the tall grass, and in the woods, under logs and in hollow trees. If he is disturbed in his nest, he will spring at the intruder like a tiger, sometimes jumping three and four feet.

On the 4th of July, we requested of the Prison Commander permission to celebrate Independence day, which he finally granted, with the promise not to allude to the *"unpleasantness"* then existing between the North and South. We assembled at 10 A. M. under our green arbors, formed by the green boughs across the whole width of the street, where a rude platform had been erected for the speakers. The exercises consisted of reading the Declaration, orations and toasts. Here were gathered the officers and men from nearly every Northern, and some from Southern States—representing, by their monograms, nearly every branch of the service. "Some wore the bugles of infantry, others the cross-sabers of cavalry or the trumpets of sharp-shooters, while the crossed-cannon represented the artillery, the turrets and shield the engineers, and gold-banded caps the navy." But the majority were without sign of rank, or uniform of any kind, being dressed in butternut, or the rebel grey. As Duganne says:

"Such effigies of garments! armless shirts and legless trousers; bits of blanket tied about the loins; such patches of every size and hue; such scarecrow figures of humanity! Their wives and mothers would not know them from the *chiffoniers* who rake out Northern gutters."

But their love for the Union and the "old flag" was as deep and fervent as ever, as was evinced by their frequent and hearty cheers during the exercises. Twice the celebration was marred by rebel interference; once by the officer of the day, who did not know that we had received the proper authority; the second time by a sergeant and a file of soldiers, who charged us with displaying the American flag. We were finally allowed to proceed with the celebration, with the warning that if a flag was displayed, the guards would open fire on the prisoners.

A few days after the celebration, about one thousand of the oldest prisoners were exchanged. Before leaving, they presented their huts and cooking utensils to the most needy prisoners.

Numerous ways were tried by the prisoners to escape. A large number succeeded in getting away by bribing the guards, while others tried tunneling, although there were many who did not have any faith in that mode of escape. Still, the work performed in digging proved beneficial, as it kept their minds and hands employed, while they forgot everything else. But very few tunnels were ever completed, so as to be of any benefit for escape. The rebels generally discovered them in time to prevent the prisoners from getting away, and always compelled those caught digging to fill the tunnel up again.

Still another way was the garbage cart. It was driven by one of the prisoners, accompanied by two guards. While the cart was being loaded with the refuse of the camp, some of the prisoners would engage the guards in a trade, while two of their number would secrete themselves in the cart and allow themselves to be covered up with the garbage; then the cart was driven to the woods and dumped, the men hiding in the brush until dark, when they would make good their escape. One day two officers were thus secreted, but when the cart started, a half-witted prisoner informed the guards. Upon being dumped, the officers were very much surprised to see the sentinels, who marched them back to prison. This ended that way of escape, known as the "New Cart-el."

After the prisoners had succeeded in getting

out of the stockade, they had a greater difficulty to surmount in evading the pack of bloodhounds, which was constantly kept at headquarters, to hunt down escaped prisoners. Three or four weeks before we arrived, fifteen officers made their escape one stormy night, but in less than forty-eight hours, thirteeen had been recaptured by the hounds. Duganne, in "Camps and Prisons," gives the following description of the last one that was retaken :

"Lieut. Collins, a fine western officer, was nearly murdered by them. He had stopped to rest, when the deep howl of dogs apprised him of pursuit. Ere he could make away, two rebels rode upon him. A brace of six-shooters were leveled at his breast, and the accustomed threat, with a huge oath, of shooting on the spot, was flung at him. "We'll give the dogs a taste of your infernal Yankee blood. Seize him ! Shake him !" The furious hounds, thus encouraged, sprang at Lieut. Collins; their glittering white teeth, with white foam gathered on their fiery gums, met in his ragged uniform. He felt the tearing of his garments, and expected momentarily to bleed ; when the rebels, with malicious laughter, called off their hounds. "You see, Yank, they'd as soon eat Yank as nigger. Now jes' tote yer carcass, Yank, or we'll shoot you on sight, by ———."

" To fully realize and appreciate these 'dogs of war,' one ought to be hunted and a fugitive, like Lieut. Collins and his compatriots. While sinking with fatigue, spent with privation, hopeless of escape, to hear the wolf-like yelp and long, hyena howl of these trained man-hunters, is something to experience. Some hounds will track a human being, day and night, for weeks, and follow his scent, especially if it be a negro, hundreds of miles, through swamps and woods and over watercourses. They are at times like game-dogs, smelling the ground at intervals, making deer-leaps, springing up to touch the overhanging leaves with their nose, they double and dart around in circles, cross a stream, and then, with a few sniffs of the air, rush up or down the bank to find their broken scent again.

"The quickness of their smell is quite as wonderful as its tenacity. When a negro or a white man is to be pursued, the dogs are simply taken to the trail and made to nose it. The real hounds are never allowed to hunt down any game inferior to man. When not in use, they are chained up and kept on starving rations. They grow fierce as tigers, with forced abstinence, and their scent becomes acute in the extreme. Woe to the hunted man, if hunger-maddened hounds overtake him in the swamps or timber, while the mounted pursuers are too far behind to call them off or moderate their savage eagerness. Woe to the fugitive if the sleuth-dogs once taste his blood!"

The rebels tried on all occasions, by misrepresentation, to make the prisoners believe that it was the fault of our Government that we were not exchanged, which, in the absence of any proof to the contrary, was accepted as the truth by many, and naturally caused some dissatisfaction. Besides, the rebels offered great inducements to our soldiers to desert. Mechanics, of all kinds, were tempted with promises of steady work at big wages; but to their credit be it said, in spite of their longing for liberty, coupled with the deprivations in prison, but few accepted these offers. One prisoner begged to be let out, on any conditions that the rebels might name. He had quarreled with his best friend about a loaf of corn bread, and in a fit of anger had struck him behind the ear with his fist, with such force that he dropped dead at his feet. He took the oath of allegiance to the Confederacy, and was let out of prison. We never heard from him afterward.

When we were captured, our color-bearer, Isaac Scott, tore the regimental flag from the staff, and gave it to his mess-mate, to conceal in his haversack. He was left sick on the way to prison, and did not arrive for some time after, but through all his sickness he clung to the flag, and upon arriving at Camp Ford, delivered it to the officers of the Regiment for safe keeping. A hole was dug inside of our shanty, in which we buried the flag. But the rebels found out, through some means, that there was a Union flag in camp. They searched for it on several occasions, but failed to discover it. To keep our large, beautiful silk flag buried, would soon have ruined it, therefore it was sewed up in Capt. Gunsaullus's blouse. He wore it among the rebels, with the flag sewed inside the lining. The flag was shown secretly to a number of prisoners, some of whom had been in captivity for nearly two years, and their eyes glistened at the sight of that "Emblem of Freedom."

The rebels furnished us with a few kettles and old axes. Everything else we had to provide ourselves, in the best way we could. For wash-tubs we made troughs ; for wash-boards we cut ridges in boards. Our army being composed of men of every trade, in a short time most of them were at work, contriving something pertaining to their several handicrafts. There was the tailor, the shoemaker, the watch-maker, the turner, with his lathe, who made chess, checkers and other articles ; and the baker, who made leather biscuits at twenty cents apiece, or a pie for a dollar. The most extensive industries were the manufacture of stools and arm-chairs, and plaiting straw for summer hats. There were also brokers, who exchanged Confederate money for coin and "Greenbacks," giving forty dollars in exchange for the former, and seven for the latter--loaning money at *fifty per cent.*, payable when exchanged. There were also dealers in tobacco, buttons, etc.

For amusements, we had chess and checkers. We also had religious services every Sabbath, as long as the chaplains remained, and prayer meetings twice a week. And last, but not least, the printer was there with his paper, called "The Camp Ford News," which was published oscasionally by Lieut. Hughes, of the 28th Iowa. The letters were made with a pen, in imitation of printers' type. The paper was quite a success, and was the source of much amusement.

Our rations, which consisted of one pint of corn meal and about half a pound of fresh beef, (salt was issued in such small quantities that it scarcely deserves mention,) were brought in every morning in bulk, and divided at the "Public Square," Capt. Joe Stevison, of the 77th Ills., superintending the thankless task very satisfactorily. His services will be kindly remembered by all. Provisions could be bought of the old planters in the vicinity, but at enormous prices—corn meal from five to eight dollars a bushel; flour two and a half dollars a pound; salt from one to two dollars a pint; bacon one dollar a pound; while coffee, sugar, butter and chickens were not in the market, except at such fabulous prices that the prisoners were unable to purchase, except in small quantities, and then not often.

One day an old citizen, accompanied by a guard, came in with a cart-load of provisions to dispose of. A crowd soon gathered around him, climbing up on his cart and mule, and filling every available space. While he was busily engaged, selling to the prisoners, who were crowding and thrusting by the handful their Confederate scrip, in exchange for his produce, some one pulled out the dumping-pin, and away went the old man, guard, gun, bacon, chickens, meal, etc., to the ground. When he regained his feet, everything had disappeared but the mule and cart. He had even lost his pocket-book and hat.

In regard to the treatment of the prisoners, it was generally bad, and in some cases brutal and even cruel to the last degree. Calvert, of the 77th Ohio, was shot by the guard, merely to try his markmanship. O. S. Shoemaker, of the 130th Illinois, formerly from near Lynchburg, Ohio, was shot through and killed, while conversing on a religious subject with a comrade. A member of the 173d New York, while running after his hat, which had blown off, was fired at by one of the guards with a shot-gun, and the entire charge lodged in his face and shoulders.

About the 10th of August, the rebel papers announced that there would be no more exchange of prisoners, on account of the difficulty concerning the exchange of negro soldiers, which naturally caused many to think about making their escape. On the 20th of August, Maj. Bering and Lieut. Srofe forged a pass, and left Camp Ford for Little Rock, Ark. The account of their adventures will be found at the close of the history of the Regiment.

The day after they made their escape, the Commander of the Prison, Col. Border, was relieved by Col. Sweet. The prisoners were all drawn up in line, preparatory to being turned over to our new commander. All who had escaped, up to this time, had been accounted for in various ways, but the number had now become too large. We therefore concluded to account only for those present, knowing that they would not find out when the absentees escaped or how long they had been gone. The first name called, of the absentees, was that of Maj. Bering. The answer was, "Taken a French." The next, Lieut. Srofe, and so on, until they found out for the first time that no less than twenty-four officers had made their escape, but had heretofore been successfully accounted for as present. At first they treated the discovery as a joke, but when it reached so large a number they were vexed, and they afterwards instructed their roll-callers not to accept the word of any prisoner for the whereabouts of an officer, but to see each in person. However, they soon found it too difficult to hunt up every one that was not present, and dropped into the old way again.

With the new commander came new guards, who were old men above fifty, taken from the rebel reserve. They were very vigilant, and escapes were less frequent.

Although a large number of the men suffered considerably with sore eyes, scurvy and dysentery, the Regiment lost but three from sickness while in prison, Moore, of Co. B, James Purdy, Co. C, and M. Nash, Co. G. This was owing in a great measure to their energy, in building huts, caves or shelters; to their long service, and the spirit of "never despair," peculiar to the Western troops.

CHAPTER XVII.

Paroled—Leaving Camp Ford—Arrival at Four-Mile Spring—Maj. Bering and Lieut. Srofe on Their Way Back to Prison—Journey to Grand Ecore—Camped at Alexandria—Arrival at the Mississippi—Exchanged—The Old Flag—New Orleans—Col. Dwight—Natchez—Provost Guard—Consolidated with the 83d Ohio—Home on Veteran Furlough.

AFTER numerous reports of exchange, at last the paroling officer, Capt. Birchett, arrived with orders from the Commissioner of Exchange to parole about seven hundred and fifty prisoners, and take them to the mouth of Red river for exchange. He selected the 19th Ky. and 48th Ohio regiments, and a number of small squads and individual members of different commands. We signed the parole on the 30th of September, 1864. The condition of the parole was not to bear arms against their government until duly exchanged.

The next day, Oct. 1st, we left Camp Ford for Shreveport, one hundred and ten miles distant, where we arrived after five days' weary march, foot-sore and tired. We camped at Four Mile Spring one week, waiting for boats to take us down Red river. While here we were granted the freedom of the camp, with the warning, that if anyone was found over one hundred yards from camp he would be sent back to prison. A few days after our arrival, we learned from Capt. Birchett, rebel paroling officer, that Maj. Bering and Lieut. Srofe had been recaptured and were at Shreveport, on their way back to prison. In a few days they passed us, with about two hundred others, on their way back to Camp Ford. They received their letters, which had arrived at Camp Ford during their absence, and proceeded on their way, looking sad and weary. But they had the sympathy of the whole Regiment, and there was many a regret that they could not accompany the Regiment on its way to freedom, instead of returning back to prison.

On the 11th of October, about half the prisoners started on foot to Grand Ecore; the other half went by boats. From there all went by steamer to Alexandria. Here we disembarked and camped until Oct. 22d, when we were again ordered aboard and taken down the stream to within a few miles of the Mississippi. Here we remained until Sunday evening, the 23d, when the boats started with us for the Mississippi, which we entered at 4 P. M. Passing down a short distance, we landed under the "stars and stripes" once more. With light hearts we stepped off the rebel craft, and were turned over to Col. Dwight, our Commissioner of Exchange. He ordered us on board the St. Mary's, where a band of music from New Orleans, and a number of ladies—

wives of Union officers—were awaiting our arrival.

We immediately boarded the vessel, and proceeded to the upper deck. The old flag was torn from its place of concealment, (Capt. Gunsaulus' blouse) and hastily tied to a staff prepared for the occasion. At this signal the band struck up the "Star-Spangled Banner," and the old flag of the 48th was unfurled to the breeze, with waving handkerchiefs and amid the wild shouts and deafening cheers of the released prisoners and groans of the rebel guards. But no words of "tongue or pen" can convey the emotions of that hour. It was an inspiring scene, and one that never will be forgotten by those who witnessed it. The flag was afterwards placed in the flag-room of the State-House at Columbus, Ohio, where it now remains.

The rebel Assistant Agent of Exchange, Capt. Birchett, on his return to Camp Ford, related to the prisoners how the flag of the 48th Ohio, in his presence, was torn from the coat of one of the officers, after they were exchanged at the mouth of Red river. He said it was one of the most exciting scenes he ever witnessed, and that the Regiment deserved a great deal of credit for preserving their colors during their imprisonment.

Soon after boarding our boat the musty corn bread and tough salt beef was thrown away, and we eagerly partook of our regular rations once more.

In the evening the rebel boats came alongside the St. Mary's, and their Commissioner of Exchange, Col. Szymanski, and Capt. Birchett, paroling officer, came aboard, to arrange with Col. Dwight for the next exchange. Here they were feasted on the best the boat afforded, by the officers of our Regiment, in the hope that they would keep their promise and include Maj. 'Bering and Lieut. Srofe in the next exchange, but it was all in vain; the promise was never fulfilled.

The rebels returned up Red river, and we proceeded to New Orleans, where we arrived the 24th. After disembarking, we were sent to the parole camp, by way of the back streets and alleys, being too ragged to be seen. Here the prisoners were furnished with new clothing, after which passes were issued, and they were allowed the freedom of the city.

The Paymaster, who had paid the remnant of the Regiment at Natchez, a short time previous, very kindly paid the officers two months' pay, which enabled them to obtain a change of clothing.

Here, with regret, we parted with the 19th Kentucky, a regiment with whom we had been associated for nearly two years. The friendly feeling which had existed between the two regiments, was manifested on all occasions. During that time we had stood side by side in every siege and battle; sharing alike victory and defeat, until now we bade them adieu. Great praise is due to such brave and patriotic men, who stood up for the Union, in the dark hours of our National existence. Although from a slave State, and many of them owning slaves, they did not hesitate to rally round the old flag at their country's call.

Shortly after the prisoners arrived at New Orleans, the officers were invited by Col. Dwight, our Commissioner of Exchange, to visit him at his office. We accepted the invitation, and met the Commissioner, who gave us a hearty welcome. After partaking of refreshments, we passed the evening in relating to him the details of our prison life in Texas. The Commissioner explained the difficulties he had encountered in making the exchange, but thought he had effected an arrangement whereby another lot of three or four hundred would be exchanged soon. He also informed us that all the exchanged prisoners would be granted a prison furlough of thirty days.

Most of the 48th were veterans, who were still entitled to their veteran furlough of "thirty days in the State," and the time of those that were not veterans had expired, therefore none of our Regiment availed themselves of the prison furlough, but remained at New Orleans until November 2d, when we were ordered to Natchez, Mississippi, where Col. Parker, with the remnant of the Regiment, was on provost-guard. We arrived on the 3d, and were welcomed back by those who escaped our fate.

Col. Parker, who had rejoined the army at

Grand Ecore, shortly after the capture of the Regiment, was put in command of the remnant of the brigade during the retreat down Red river. They were finally sent to New Orleans, where the Colonel, in the latter part of July, obtained furloughs for the veterans of the Regiment who had escaped capture, and those who had rejoined from sick-leave and detached duty, and took them home. Before leaving, they procured quite a gay uniform, in which they made a handsome appearance. Upon arriving at Cincinnati they were paraded through the streets to the Fifth Street Barracks, where they were quartered.

The following editorial appeared in the Cincinnati Times, of August 4th, 1864:

"THE BRAVE 48TH OHIO.

"This noble Regiment, all that is left of it—ninety-four men—arrived in the city yesterday morning, and marched to the Fifth Street Barracks. They come home as re-enlisted veterans, to enjoy their thirty days' furlough, and then return to the field of strife. Three years since, the 48th left Camp Dennison, 960 strong. It returns to us ninety-four men, all the rest being wounded, prisoners, or among the gallant dead. During the late Red River Expedition, this Regiment lost 190 of its few remaining men, and every one of its commissioned officers, with the exception of its Colonel, one Captain and one Lieutenant. Previous to leaving New Orleans, the furloughed men fitted themselves out with an elegant and peculiar uniform. They leave to-day for their homes. Col. J. R. Parker, who commands this organization, has good cause to be proud of it."

While at home, they obtained eighty new recruits, and on their way back to New Orleans, their boat was fired into by guerrillas, which mortally wounded W. H. Osborn, of Co. B, and S. H. Raper, of Co. K. This occurred a short distance above Vicksburg. They were left at the hospital at that place, where they died soon after.

Upon arriving at New Orleans, they were assigned the duty of guarding the rebel prisoners, who were confined in the cotton presses. They were relieved from this duty by the remnant of the 77th Ills., and moved up to Natchez, Miss., on the steamer "Jennie Rogers," where they arrived on the 14th of October. They relieved the 29th Ills., who were on provost-guard, and occupied the Court House as quarters, when we rejoined them at Natchez. The Reg't. remained on provost-duty, occasionally going out on picket, until Nov. 19th, when the 48th Ohio, 97th Ills., 69th Ind., and 26th Ohio Battery, under command of Col. Parker, were ordered on a scouting expedition, on the Woodville road.

Rainy weather set in, and the roads becoming impassable for the artillery to proceed, the expedition was abandoned after a few days absence, and we returned to camp, bringing all the forage the teams could haul.

After two unsuccessful attempts to obtain our veteran furlough, at last the necessary papers were forwarded to Memphis, Tenn., for the approval of the Commanding General.

On the first of January, 1865, we received orders from Gen. Canby, through Gen. Brayman, Commander of the Post, consolidating our Regiment with the 83d Ohio. The following is a copy :

"HEADQUARTERS MILITARY DIVISION,
WEST MISS., NEW ORLEANS, LA.,
December 26, 1864.

EXTRACT.

"Special Orders, No. 224.

* * * * * * * *

"VI. Under the provisions of General Order No. 86, series of 1863, War Department, Adjutant General's Office, the following named regiments will be consolidated, viz : 48th Ohio Vet. Vol. Infantry; 83d Ohio Vol. Infantry.

"VII. The Battalions of the 48th and 83d Ohio Volunteer Infantry will be consolidated into ten companies, to be designated as the 83d Ohio Volunteer Infantry. All supernumeraries, commissioned and non-commissioned officers, will be mustered out as of date of the consolidation. Brig. Gen'l. Brayman, Commanding District of Natchez, is charged with the execution of this order. * *

"By command of MAJ. GEN. CANBY.
"C. F. CHRISTENSEN, Lt. Col. & A. A. G."

This order did not take effect until the 17th of

January, 1865. The ten companies of the 48th Ohio were consolidated into four, and those of the 83d Ohio into six companies. The field officers of the 83d were retained, mustering out of service the following officers of the 48th Ohio : Col. J. R. Parker, Lieut. Col. J. W. Lindsay; Captains Cyrus Hussey, James Sowry and Thomas Montgomery; Lieut. H. W. Day, Hospital Steward Jos. H. Gravatt, and Serg't. Maj. W. A. Pratt, and all supernumerary non-commissioned officers of each company. Maj. J. A. Bering was included in the muster-out, but being confined in prison, he was not mustered out until after his release, June 16, 1865. The companies lost their identity after the consolidation.

This order of consolidation was an act of injustice to the Regiment, for we were promised the continuation of the organization through the war on account of two thirds re-enlisting, and the officers and men regarded it as showing bad faith on the part of the Government.

Company E, which had been the color-company during the entire service, delivered the flag of the Regiment to Col. Parker, who brought it home and retained possession of it until his death, which took place December 5, 1865. Mrs. Parker, upon the request of the members of Company A, delivered the flag to E. T. Rayburn, of New Lexington, Highland county, Ohio, where it still remains.

On the 5th of January, 1865, the prison veterans received their long-promised furlough, and started on the first steamer for home. We arrived at Cairo on the evening of the 10th, and Cincinnati at 4 A. M. on the 12th, after an absence of over three years. Upon receiving transportation, the members of the Regiment separated for their respective homes, where the old Veterans received a merited hearty welcome from their friends, which was one continued feast and ovation until they returned to active service again.

CHAPTER XVIII.

Preparation for Active Service Again—Brigaded with Colored Troops—Embarking for New Orleans—Arrival at Barrancas, Fla.—Prison Veterans Rejoin from Furlough—Pensacola—Fort Blakely Invested—The Charge and Capture—Up the Alabama River—Selma—Return to Mobile—Explosion of Rebel Ammunition—Ordered to Texas—Arrival at Galveston—Mustered Out of the 83d Ohio—The Old 48th Ohio Itself Again—Ordered to Houston—Break-Bone Fever—Back to Galveston—Promotions—On Various Duties—Final Muster-Out—Arrival at Columbus—Home and a Quiet Life—Reid's History of the 48th Ohio—Testimonials of Brigade and Division Commanders.

THE incidents and adventures of the Regiment, from the consolidation until the close of the war and final muster-out, were furnished by Lieut. James Douglas, of Mt. Auburn, Cincinnati, who was a member of the Regiment, and served the entire term.

"Immediately after the consolidation, the Regiment was brigaded with the 77th and 58th U. S. Colored Troops, and went into camp on the Quitman farm, back of the city, under command of Brig. Gen. Davidson. On the 28th of January, orders came to break camp and embark on the steamer Grey Eagle. This was accomplished by midnight. The following day found us going down the Mississippi, en route for New Orleans. On the 30th we disembarked at the lower part of the city, near the Lake Pontchartrain depot. We boarded the train, which took us to Lakeport. There we embarked on the ocean steamer "Alabama," and midnight of the same day found our vessel steaming down Lake Pontchartrain. On the 31st, we passed through Lake Borgne, thence into Mississippi Sound, making a short stop at Pensacola, Fla. From there into the Gulf, finally landing at Barrancas, opposite Ft. Pickens, Fla., on the 1st day of February, at which place we disembarked and went into camp, forming a part of the 3d Brigade, 2d Division 13th A. C., which composed a part of the right wing of the army moving against the defenses of Mobile. The Brigade was commanded by Col. F. W. More, of the 83d Ohio, which left Lieut. Col. W. H. Baldwin in command of the Regiment. We remained at Barrancas, Fla., some time, organizing and preparing for an active campaign. While here, the Prison Veterans rejoined from their furlough, and were assigned to their respective companies, under the new organization.

"On the 10th of March, we broke camp and marched around a portion of Pensacola Bay, to Pensacola, where we arrived the same day and went into camp near the railroad. We remained in camp until the 20th of February, when we again took up the line of march, moving up the Montgomery railroad, through the pine swamp, in a northerly direction. The campaign will be remembered by those engaged in it, as it differed from any previous one. The route lay through almost impassable pine swamps. The men carried 80 rounds of ammunition, an ax to every fourth man, an extra pair of shoes, and ten days' rations each. The ground was of a quicksand nature, and we were frequently obliged to pull wagons and mules out with long ropes. We cut down trees, and built miles of corduroy roads at the worst places. It was slow marching, with constant fatigue duties, lasting far into the night. To make matters worse, the first night out from Pensacola, a violent rain-storm set in, damaging the provisions we carried, and after our ten days were up we were placed on one-fourth rations.

"On the 26th our advance met the enemy at Escambia river, defeating them, and capturing 120 rebels and the rebel Gen. Clayton, who was wounded. We captured Pollard also, a railroad junction, two trains of cars, a rebel paymaster, and some more prisoners. After this our route lay due west, but the roads were not much better. We arrived at Stockton on the 31st of March, and the 2d of April found us driving the rebel skirmishers into their works at Fort Blakely, Ala.

" It was a beautiful day. The troops were all brought to the front, and preparations made for a charge. We formed *en masse*, one brigade directly in the rear of the other, thus forming a solid column. Extra ammunition was distributed, and the musicians were formed into a hospital corps, with stretchers. In this position we stacked arms, under a heavy artillery fire from the enemy.

"While thus waiting in suspense, an order came to change our position, and towards evening our Division moved to the left, in the woods, occupying the center of the army. The following day we began to invest Fort Blakely, driving the enemy closer to their works, our Regiment taking a position in a ravine, where we remained until the final charge, in the meantime performing constant fatigue and picket duty, resembling those duties at Vicksburg, only we were not so well protected.

"On the 9th of April we were formed in line of battle in our rifle-pits. One regiment from each brigade was selected to deploy as skirmishers; our Regiment being selected from our brigade. Owing to the formation of the ground, we marched left in front. It was a grand sight to see the vast army, prepared for a charge. Word was passed along the line for the skirmishers to advance at the bugle signal, and the main line to advance, if necessary, when the bugle sounded. We advanced in skirmish order, a distance of 500 yards, under a heavy fire of artillery, and a musketry cross-fire, over fallen timber, sunken torpedoes, and a double line of strong abattis works, going through and over the rebel forts, in the face of a deadly fire, without the assistance of the reserve, although they were ready to support us if we failed. The rebel gunners left some of their pieces partly loaded. Some of the rebels surrendered and others fled. The Regiment captured two forts, eight cannon, two mortars, a long line of breastworks, eight hundred prisoners, two flags, and a large quantity of small arms, ammunition and other stores. The colors were riddled, both staffs were shot in two, but the color-bearers gallantly carried the flags over the parapet of the fort. The Regiment lost 36 officers and men, in killed and wounded.

"This victory gave us possession of Mobile and its defenses, and cut the Confederacy in two. We remained at Fort Blakely until the 20th of April, when we embarked and moved across to Mobile, at which place we formed a part of a fleet moving up the Alabama river. The army was divided into three columns, the 16th Corps and Grierson's cavalry moving north from Fort Blakely to Montgomery, Ala., Gen. Benton's Division, 13th A. C., moving north up the railroad, and our Division, under Gen. Anderson, and Hawkins' Colored Division, moving up the river in a fleet of transports. Our Regiment embarked seven companies on the "Gov. Cowels," and the other three on the "St. Charles," the latter a rebel blockade-runner.

"We had a very pleasant time going up the river. We were allowed plenty of liberty, the country was rich in provisions, and we made use of it. We were fired into once, and retaliated. This was the last time the Regiment was fired at. On the 27th of April we reached Selma, Ala., and went into camp near the grave-yard, just inside the rebel works. The cavalry, under Gen. Wilson, had previously captured the place and destroyed a vast amount of ordnance stores and manufactories.

"We were in Selma until the 12th of May, when we embarked on the steamer "John H. Groesbeck," and proceeded to Mobile. We performed provost-duty at that place for some time. On the 2d of May, the Governor promoted Lieut. McCaffrey to Captain, and Second Lieut. J. M. Wilson to First Lieutenant. During our stay the rebel ammunition stored near the depot exploded, which caused much damage to property and the loss of many lives, some of our Regiment among the number.

"On the 13th of June, the Regiment embarked on the ocean steamer "J. T. Rice," with orders to proceed to Texas. We passed Forts Morgan and Gaines, thence into the Gulf of Mexico, encountering some storms, and arriving at Galveston, Texas, on the 18th. After disembarking, we camped in the public square, but shortly afterward broke camp. Each company was assigned to different parts of the city, occupying dwelling-houses for quarters. Soon after arriving at Galveston, an order was received, to muster out all troops whose term of service expired previous to October 1st, 1865. Under this order the original 83d O. V. I. was mustered out July 26th, 1865, when they departed for home. Under this order also, quite a number of the 48th were discharged, and at the same time we received accessions from other regiments, of men whose term of service did not expire with their regiments.

"Under Special Orders No. 48, 13th A. C., dated July 19, 1865, the Regiment resumed its old name of 48th Ohio Vet. Vol. Infantry, and was placed under command of Capt. J. R. Lynch, afterward promoted to Lieut.-Col. Lieut. W. H. H. Rike was assigned as Adjutant, Lieut. W. J. Srofe as Quartermaster, Surgeon P. A. Willis as Surgeon, and H. Baird as Ass't Surgeon. The latter was from the 114th Ohio. Serg't. James Douglas was appointed Serg't.-Major, and William C. Edwards was appointed Hospital Steward. Ass't. Surgeon C. H. Wiles and Lieut. Reed were discharged the latter part of July.

"On the 2d day of August, a portion of the Regiment embarked and proceeded to Houston, Texas, by way of Buffalo Bayou. The remaining companies followed soon after, by way of Trinity river. Arriving at Houston, we relieved the 34th Iowa, who were to be mustered out. Lieut.-Col. Lynch relieved Col. Clark as Commander of the Post. Lieut. McCaffrey was appointed Post-Adj't. and Lieut. Srofe, Post-Quartermaster.

"The Regiment was now sent by companies to various towns on the railroads running into Houston. Capt. Cochran, with Company C, was stationed at Columbia, on the Brazos river, 85 miles from Houston. While stationed there they buried the brother of President Johnson, who had been fatally injured while boating. The company also lost two of its men from malarial fever.

"During the summer the Regiment suffered from break-bone fever, causing many to be sick. At one time it was difficult to provide guards for duty. It was not, however, fatal to any of them.

"On the 28th of October, we were relieved from duty at Houston, and ordered to relieve the 24th Ind. Vet. Vols. from duty at Galveston, who were then being mustered out of service. In due time we reached Galveston, and took possession of their comfortable quarters.

"On the 4th of September, 1865, the Governor issued the following commissions: Lieut. Rike, promoted to Captain; Sergeants S. H. Stevenson, B. W. Ladd, and F. N. Sweny, promoted to 1st Lieutenants, and Sergeants Asa N. Ballard, Elihu Hiatt, Q. M. Sergt. Thos. H. Hansell and Serg't. Maj. James Douglas, promoted to 2d Lieutenants. Lieut. Stevenson was appointed Adjutant in place of Lieut. Rike, promoted. H. J. Rausman was appointed Q. M. Serg't. Oct. 5, 1865.

"From the time the Regiment returned to Galveston, in October, 1865, until our muster-out, we performed all kinds of garrison duty, and the officers were more or less on detached service, but we were not well satisfied with our situation or treatment, for we felt that we were detained in the service longer than was actually necessary. In fact, many expressed themselves in such a way as to leave no doubt of the feelings of the Regiment.

"On the 23d of April, we received orders for our final muster-out, which was completed, so that we were enabled to leave Galveston on the 11th day of May, 1866, arriving at Columbus, Ohio, May 21st, 1866."

Thus ended the existence of the 48th Ohio Vet. Vol. Infantry, after a service of nearly five years, having traveled during that time through eight Southern States, a distance by land and water of eleven thousand five hundred miles, and being next to the last Ohio Infantry Regiment discharged from the service.

The following is what Reid says of the 48th Ohio, in "Ohio in the War:"

"This Regiment was organized at Camp Dennison on the 17th of February, 1862, and soon after reported to Gen. W. T. Sherman, at Paducah, Kentucky. After a short rest at Paducah, it moved up the Tennessee River, on the steamer Empress, and on the 19th of March disembarked at Pittsburg Landing. On the 4th of April, while the regiment was on drill, firing was heard, and the 48th at once moved in the direction of the sound; but the enemy fell back, and at night-fall the regiment returned to its quarters. About 7 o'clock on the morning of the 6th, the regiment advanced upon the enemy, and was soon warmly engaged. Charge after charge was repulsed, and though the rebel fire was making fearful gaps in the line, the men stood firm. A battery was sent to the regiment's aid, but after firing four shots, it retired. The rebels then advanced, confidently expecting to capture the regiment, but were driven back, and the 48th withdrew to its supports, having been ordered three times by Gen. Sherman to fall back. It is claimed that Gen. Johnston, of the rebel army, was killed in this portion of the battle, by some member of the 48th. The regiment was actively engaged during the remainder of the day, and late in the afternoon, in connection with the 24th Ohio and 36th Indiana, it participated in a decisive attack on the rebel lines. It acted throughout in Buckland's Brigade of Sherman's Division—a Brigade which had no share in the early rout of a part of that Division.

"On the second day of the battle, about 10 o'clock A. M., the regiment went into action across an open field, under a galling fire, and continued constantly exposed until the close of the engagement. The 48th lost about one-third of its members in this battle. From this time until after the close of the Rebellion, the regiment was engaged continually in active duty. In the attack upon Corinth, the 48th was among the first organized troops to enter the rebel works. In Gen. Sherman's first expedition to Vicksburg, it occupied, with credit, a position on the right in the assault; and it was in Sherman's expedition up the Arkansas River, that it distinguished itself in the battle of Arkansas Post. It was with Grant during his Vicksburg campaign; fought at Magnolia Hills and

Champion Hills, and participated in a general assault on the rebel works in the rear of Vicksburg, May 22d, 1863.

"On the 25th of June following, another assault was made upon the same works, and the 48th was ordered to cross an open field, exposed to two enfilading batteries, to take position in the advanced line of rifle-pits, and to pick off the enemy's gunners. This order was successfully executed. It took a prominent part in the battle of Jackson, Mississippi, and soon after engaged in the fight at Bayou Teche. At Sabine Cross-Roads, the 48th, then a mere remnant of its former self, severely punished the "Crescent Regiment;" but in turn it was overpowered and captured. It was not exchanged until October, 1864.

"The majority of the men in the regiment re-enlisted, but on account of the capture, they never received their veteran furlough. After its exchange, the regiment shared in the capture of Mobile.

"After the surrender of the rebel armies, the remaining one hundred and sixty-five men of this regiment were ordered to Texas. The regiment was at last mustered out of service in May, 1866."

The following testimonials were received from our Division and Brigade Commanders, in regard to the conduct of the 48th while under their immediate command :

"HEADQUARTERS, ARMY OF THE UNITED
"STATES, WASHINGTON, D. C.,
"March 26th, 1880.

"*Maj. J. A. Bering and Capt. Thomas Montgomery:*

"DEAR SIRS:—I am really indebted to you for the pleasure of having the opportunity to read your beginning of the "History of the Forty-Eighth Ohio Volunteer Infantry," and wish to encourage you to go on in the same spirit to the end.

"I recognize in every page that the writer was one of us, that he saw with the eyes of a brave, intelligent soldier, who meant to do his full share of work, and who now only intends to record his observations for the use of his comrades, and to furnish authentic materials for the future historians of the great events in which the 48th Ohio bore an honorable part.

"I prefer not to be a critic, to alter or change a single paragraph, because I believe the great end at which we all aim, Truth, is best reached by each witness telling his own story in his own way.

"War consists not only in absolute facts, which ought to be absolutely correct, but in feelings and opinions at the moment of action, because these account for results. I advise you to go on to the conclusion in the same spirit you began, and I am sure your comrades will be grateful, and the cause for which we fought will be vindicated by future generations.

"With great respect, your friend,
"W. T. SHERMAN, General."

"WASHINGTON, D. C., April 7, 1880.
"*Maj. J. A. Bering and Capt. Thomas Montgomery*:
"GENTLEMEN:—I have received your letter of the 1st inst., also the one hundred pages of your History of the 48th Ohio has come to hand, and been read with a great deal of interest, as far as it is continued. My old Brigade, consisting of the 48th, 53d, 70th and 72d Regiments Ohio Volunteer Infantry, I had always regarded as equal, in all respects, to any brigade I ever met with. It affords me great pleasure to say, that during the time the regiment was in my command, its conduct was excellent. Indeed it has afforded me a great pleasure, at all times, to speak in terms of high commendation of the officers and men of the 48th. The discipline and general conduct of the Regiment was good, and my personal relations with them, the officers and men, were of such a character that it has always been a sincere pleasure to me to meet one of them.

"I have the honor to be, very respectfully,
"Your obedient servant,
"J. W. DENVER,
"Brig. Gen. U. S. Vols."

"FREMONT, OHIO, April 5, 1880.
"*Major J. A. Bering and Capt. Thomas Montgomery:*

"GENTLEMEN:—I have the honor to acknowledge the receipt of your esteemed favor of the 24th ult., and also the first one hundred pages of your forthcoming " History of the 48th Ohio. " I have read those pages with great interest and satisfaction, and I take great pleasure in bearing testimony to the uniform good conduct and unwavering valor of the 48th Ohio, both officers and privates, that composed a part of the Brigade which I had the honor of commanding. All the incidents and circumstances of the commencement and progress of the terrible battle of Shiloh, are still fresh in my memory. At the first alarm, our Brigade was ordered to form on the color-line, and I rode forward to the picket-line and found the enemy advancing in strong force, driving our pickets. I immediately rode back through our Brigade-line to Gen. Sherman's Headquarters, and informed him that I had been to the front and found the enemy advancing in great force and our pickets falling back, and asked him what orders he had to give me. He answered: " You must reinforce the pickets and keep the enemy back. " On my return, I met Col. Sullivan and Lieut. Col. Parker, of the 48th Ohio, riding to meet me, and when I informed them what my orders were, they both asked permission to take the 48th to the front, which I readily assented to, and directed them to march their Regiment with as much speed as possible across the bridge immediately in front of the Regiment, which was done with the utmost promptness. But, as stated in your History, the enemy were already forming a line on our side of the creek, below the bridge, concealed from our view by the high bank. The whole Brigade was at once advanced, and the battle commenced in deadly earnest all along the line. No more courageous fighting was ever done than was done by the 48th, 70th and 72d Ohio regiments during the next two hours. We drove the enemy back repeatedly, and held our line until ordered back to the Purdy road. I do not think our Brigade has ever received from the public the credit it deserved for that first two hours' fight.

"Although our ranks were constantly being terribly cut to pieces, there was no flinching in the officers or privates. We were ordered by Gen. Sherman to hold our position, and were determined to do it, and did, until ordered back. I consider it the greatest honor of my life that I commanded the Fourth Brigade in Gen. Sherman's division, composed of the 48th, 70th and 72d Ohio regiments, at the great battle of Shiloh. No braver men ever defended their country on the battlefield. I am, with great respect,
 "Your sincere friend,
 "R P. BUCKLAND,
 "Brig. Gen. U. S. Vols."

"LANCASTER, KY., Feb. 6, 1880.
"*Maj. J. A. Bering and Capt. Thos. Montgomery:*

"I regret that it is not in my power to furnish copies of my official reports of the engagements in which my brigade participated during the war. The 48th Ohio was assigned to my command at Memphis, Tenn., in December, 1862, and composed a part of my brigade until after the Red River campaign. It participated in the movement under Gen. W. T. Sherman against Chickasaw Bayou, in front of Vicksburg, at Arkansas Post, and under Gen. Grant at Port Gibson, Baker's Creek, Black River Bridge, the sieges of Vicksburg and Jackson, and under Gen. T. E. G. Ransom, at the battle of Sabine Cross-Roads. In all of the engagements named herein, no regiment of which I have any knowledge, during the late war, bore a more honorable or conspicuous part than the 48th Ohio. It was a regiment upon which I could depend at all times, and under all circumstances, for just what was needed. It was under excellent discipline, and always ready at a moment's warning, to drill, march, or fight. I had no trouble with either officers or men, and do not remember an unpleasant word that ever passed between myself and any of that command.

"At the siege of Vicksburg, on the 22d of May, they were among the first to reach the intrenchments of the enemy, and planted their flag by the side of the 77th and 130th Illinois, upon the Confederate works; which portion they held until recalled late at night, by order of the Corps Commander. I was always proud of the Regiment, and thankful to Gen. A. J. Smith, for giving me a command composed of such splendid material. Ohio, Illinois and Kentucky stood side by side, and it was a noticeable fact, that whenever the enemy got in our way, some of them were sure to get hurt, unless they managed to get out of it very soon. I always tried hard to take good care of the men, and have them ready for any emergency ; and I think the reports of the Division, Corps, and Army commanders, will show that the old second brigade of Gen. A. J. Smith's Division, made a very creditable record in the grand old Army of the Tennessee.

"Very truly yours,
"W. J. LANDRUM,
"Brevet-Brig.-Gen. U. S. Vols."

THE
ESCAPE AND RE-CAPTURE

OF

MAJ. J. A. BERING, AND LIEUT. W. J. SROFE,

WITH

PRISON LIFE

AT CAMP FORD, TEXAS,

FROM OCT. 12TH, 1864, TO MAY 17TH, 1865,

AND

THE CLOSING SCENES OF THE WAR WEST OF THE MISSISSIPPI RIVER.

By J. A. BERING,
LATE MAJOR 48TH REG'T. OHIO VOLS.

The Escape and Re-Capture.

CHAPTER I.

THE ESCAPE.

Preparing Rations—The Forged Pass—Concealed in Sight of Prison—" Ten O'Clock and All's Well "—Crossing the Sabine River—Crossing the Bridge at the Mill—The Blood-Hounds on Our Trail—Run Into a Trap—Hounds Baffled—Escape—Man with a Gun—Passing Around a Village—An All Night Tramp—Moonlight View of the Country—Hounds on the Trail Again—Narrow Escape from the Hounds—Parching Corn Under Difficulties—Lost in a Dark Swamp—Waiting for the Moon to Rise.

THE Regiment had served four months in prison since our capture, and the month of August, with its hot and sultry days, had arrived, which, with the smoke of the hundreds of fires, made the over-crowded prison-pen ten fold more uncomfortable than during the preceding months. Up to this time we had submitted to our fate with a calm resignation, for the reason that we had received our daily allowance of favorable exchange rumors, (received principally via " grape-vine lines,") but faint hearts began to complain of " hope deferred," when the rebel papers brought the cheering intelligence that, "owing to the difficulty in regard to the exchange of negro soldiers, there would be no more exchange of prisoners." The prospect of a speedy exchange was all that induced me to remain in Camp Ford, but my last hope had now departed; therefore my mind was speedily made up to leave the prison at the first favorable opportunity. After a consultation with Lieut. W. J. Srofe, of my Regiment, we agreed to undertake the trip together. We had, however, scarcely made the preliminary arrangements for the journey, when we received the information that the rebels were going to send us hundreds of miles into the interior of Texas, and they did partly execute the threat by sending 600 of our number to Hempstead, 250 miles south-west. This event nerved us up to prompt action, but we had a difficult task before us, as many re-captured Union soldiers can testify.

At prison headquarters they kept a pack of bloodhounds, with which they circled around the stockade, if they discovered that any one had escaped. But, even if successful in getting away from the prison hounds, we had to travel hundreds of miles to our lines, through a strange and hostile country; yet, in spite of all these difficulties and disadvantages we were determined to make an effort to gain our liberty, let the consequences be what they might.

Before that important step could be taken, a great many arrangements had to be made. We had to procure butternut clothes to wear, in order to pass for rebel soldiers, when necessary. We also had our maps of the country to copy; to bake crackers, dry our beef, etc., until about the 17th of August, when everything was in readiness. The route that we considered the most favorable was to strike for Little Rock, Ark., distant 300 miles north-east.

We then made arrangements with Robert Barnett, of my Regiment, (who was a kind of trader and smuggler between us and the guards,) to bribe a sentry to let us out after night. I did not like the idea of getting out in that manner, but that seemed to be our only chance. My plan was to forge a pass and go out, but that week no one was permitted to go out of the stockade, pass or no pass; therefore, the only feasible plan was to bribe a guard to let us out after night.

Barnett succeeded in making arrangements for us two or three nights in succession, but when the time came for action, the guards had either been removed, or they were watched so closely that we could not carry out our plan. At the same time I felt rather uncomfortable, when I reflected upon the idea of trusting myself in a rebel's hands. I was afraid of treachery, as they had, on several occasions, accepted bribes to let prisoners out, and when they had their pay, they would fire on those whose bribes they had taken.

On the morning of the 20th, the Colonel commanding issued passes again, to let a few out at a time. I borrowed one, and hastily made an exact copy of it. The most difficult matter now was to get our two haversacks, filled with dried beef and crackers, outside of the prison, as we dared not be seen with them when we were ready to leave. The custom of the prison commander was to let ten men out each day with the wood-wagon, to cut and load the fuel that was hauled into the stockade. They had to give their parole that they would not escape while at work.

The men that were to go out that day were members of Lieut. Srofe's company, and he arranged to go out with them. When they were ready to start, they came to our shanty, and we gave each one of them a portion of our provisions, which they hid about their persons. After they arrived in the woods, our rations were put in the haversacks and hid in a tree-top, about half a mile east from the prison. At noon, Lieut. Srofe returned with his party, and after partaking of a hasty dinner, we bade farewell to our most intimate friends, who knew our plans, and started for the prison-gate. On presenting our pass to the sentinel, Lieut. Srofe and myself were permitted to pass out of the stockade.

We had decided beforehand, that if we succeeded in getting out, we would go to the prison hospital, which was about a quarter of a mile west of the stockade, in charge of our own nurses, and remain there until evening. To reach the hospital, we had to pass by the quarters of the prison commander. He was sitting in front of his office as we passed by, but he was not aware how we got out. We were scarcely out of sight, however, when he sent orders to the guards not to allow any more out that day, whether they had passes or not. He supposed his adjutant had issued too many passes for one day. After reaching the hospital, by the advice of a slave, we procured two large pieces of soap, to rub our feet with, if the hounds should get on our track. We did not consider it safe to remain in the hospital until evening, therefore decided to go into the woods and conceal ourselves until night. We selected a place near a large field, about one mile west of the prison, and hid in the brush until dark.

We now had a difficult task to perform, to circle around the rebel camp and find our rations, which Lieut. Srofe had hid that morning, half a mile east of the prison, and at the same time avoid the rebel pickets, stationed around in the woods. We succeeded in passing around the rebel camp, where about 600 Confederate guards were quartered, without meeting with any accident.

We were guided altogether by the noise from the prison, which sounded like the hum of a large city. When we reached the neighborhood in which Lieut. Srofe thought he had concealed the provisions, we began to search for our haversacks, but there were many tree-tops lying around, and it being very dark, it was a difficult task to find the right one. The guards at the prison called out: "Eight o'clock, and all's well," and then "Nine o'clock, and all's well," and still we had not found our rations. We began to get discouraged, although we knew that we could not be a great distance from them, for the reason that we had found some of the crackers which had been dropped in the morning. After a short rest we began the search again, and just as the guards called out, "Ten o'clock, and all's well," Lieut. Srofe called me, saying: "I have found our haversacks."

We were so overjoyed at finding our provisions, that we did not hear any one coming up behind us, until they were so near that we could not run and hide, but dropped flat on the ground as quick as possible. The next moment two men on horseback galloped by, not more than ten feet from where we lay. After procuring our rations, we went to a small stream near by, and ate our supper.

We were now ready for a three hundred mile tramp, which finally turned out to be nearer six hundred. Each one had a butternut suit and a haversack, and between us, one case-knife, one tin cup, one tin plate, for parching corn, one box of matches, pencil and paper, to keep a diary of our travels. Each of us also had a map of Texas and Arkansas, which we had copied.

After finishing our supper, we traced up the north star, and took a north-east course for the land of freedom; but we soon found traveling through the dark woods, with only the stars to guide us, slow and tedious. After traveling two or three miles, we struck a creek bottom, covered with vines, briars and fallen timber. Our clothes received rough handling, and the north star was not to be seen very often, through the tall pines. Our first object now was to get out of the woods into the cleared land, or on a road, as we were now well convinced that little progress could be made by traveling through the forest at night. After searching around for two or three hours, we struck a path which led us into one of the main roads, and fortunately it ran north-east. There was nothing now to prevent us from making rapid progress on our journey.

During the night we passed six plantations; but being afraid to pass by them on the road, we circled around to the rear of the houses, and then struck the road again. When we arrived at the seventh, it was near daylight, and being considerably worn out, we passed around to a piece of timber in the rear of the buildings, then hid under some bushes in a fence-corner, and laid down on the ground to sleep. We supposed we had traveled about eleven miles during the night, and were now about that distance from the stockade.

All of our subsequent calculations in regard to the distance traveled, were based on our three years experience of marching in the army, and by referring to our maps, when we came to large streams. How near correct our estimates were of the distance traveled, will be shown at the end of the journey.

When we awoke in the morning, Sunday, Aug. 21st, we were very chilly, as it was foggy and damp. We built a fire, parched some corn, and ate breakfast. We thought it best to commence on parched corn, the first day, to save our dried beef and crackers. At about 8 o'clock, A. M., we heard the voices of some persons coming toward us. We began to get uneasy; nearer and nearer they came; I raised up cautiously and looked around, when I saw a man, woman, and a little boy, coming directly toward us.

It was too late to get away, so we gave up our cause as lost. I kept my eyes on them until they were nearly opposite us, walking along a path about fifteen feet from where we were concealed. I gave up all hope of escape, and buried my face in my hands. It was hard to give up so soon. But strange to say, they passed by without seeing us, and after they had passed a short distance, they turned to the fence, and commenced picking wild grapes, and talking very busily the whole time. As soon as they were out of sight, we gathered up our haversacks and ran into the woods, and hid in the underbrush.

Our night's travel and morning adventure convinced us that the task we had before us was beset with danger and difficulties, and that it would require all our cunning, energy and patience, to be successful in our undertaking. That Sunday proved to be a very long day to us. We conversed with each other, but not above a whisper; tried to sleep, but could not—too much excitement. We found it very tiresome to remain in one place all day, we therefore concluded to travel in the day time after that, by traveling only in the woods and keeping a sharp look-out for any one that happened to be abroad.

In the evening we left our hiding-place, and in a short time struck the same road that we had turned off from in the morning. We followed it until about nine o'clock, P. M., when we came to a mill, where the road crossed the creek on a bridge which was attached to the mill. We heard persons talking within, therefore did not venture too near, but turned off to the right in a heavy-timbered bottom, thinking that we could circle around it to avoid crossing on the bridge. After trying in vain for about an hour to make the circuit, we came back very cautiously and crossed on the bridge.

At about eleven o'clock, P. M., we reached Sabine river. We rolled a log into the stream, then one of us would get at one end of the log and swim to the opposite shore with it, while the other would hold to the log with one hand, and with the other hold our provisions out of the water. We made five trips before we had our clothes and rations over. After we had crossed, we had some difficulty in passing around some persons that were camped by the roadside. At about two o'clock, A. M., we turned off into the woods to remain until daylight—distance traveled, twelve miles.

August 22d, at daybreak, we were awakened by the yelping of hounds on our track. We sprang to our feet, grasped our haversacks and started off at the top of our speed. At one time we thought that they had lost our trail, but we soon discovered that we were very much mistaken. About every half-hour we would rub soap on the bottom of our shoes, and on the grass. Whenever they reached such a spot, it checked them for some time. The race continued until about eleven o'clock, A. M., when we came to a small piece of woods in the shape of a triangle, with cleared land all around it, excepting one of the angles that joined the woods we were in, and a number of buildings on the opposite side. Not knowing what was ahead of us, we entered this piece of timber; but we soon found that we could not cross the fields in sight of the houses, and to return the way we came would take us back towards the hounds, who were now gaining on us fast. We had, unknowingly, run into a trap. To pass by the houses was certain capture, or to turn back the way we came in, and get over into the adjoining woods, was equally hazardous, but we had no time to lose, and our only hope seemed to be to get back into the main woods before the hounds cut off our retreat. We started back, running at full speed, to reach the entrance before the hounds. It was like running into our own destruction, and at every yelp of the hounds, my heart thumped so loud that I thought I could almost hear it. Fortunately, we gained the entrance first, but had scarcely entered the adjoining woods, when the whole pack of hounds went howling into the piece of timber that we had just left, and the hunters on horseback, yelling, brought up the rear. We heard the dogs for some time afterward, but did not know whether they followed us any longer or not. No doubt they thought we were concealed about the negro quarters, and searched for us until they became tired, and then gave up the chase.

In the afternoon we concluded to halt and take a rest, as we were nearly exhausted, having traveled about fifteen miles on a run, since daylight, and not tasted anything since the evening before. We built a fire and parched some corn, and after a few hours rest we started again. One would generally take the lead, and keep the direction of the sun, while the other followed, a short distance behind. Towards evening, after crossing a small stream, we struck a road that led north-east, so we concluded to wait until night, then follow it.

As soon as it was sufficiently dark to venture out, we pursued our journey until we came to a road that we thought ran more directly north-east than the one we were on. We turned off and followed it for about half a mile, when it terminated at a plantation. We then circled completely around the buildings, but the road was nowhere to be found, which convinced us that it was only a private road, leading to the plantation. Turning back, we took the main road again, and traveled until towards morning, then turned off into the woods to rest; distance traveled that day, twenty-five miles.

August 23d, we started at daylight and traveled but a short distance, when we hid in a tree-top for the day. Some noisy children came into the woods and routed us out several times, but they did not discover us. We left at dark, and met two persons early in the evening, but concealed ourselves before they discovered us. Soon afterward, a man on horseback, with a gun in his hands, galloped furiously by. He came on us so suddenly that there was no time to hide; we therefore dropped flat on the ground by the road-side until he had passed.

The road which we were on did not suit us, as it ran in every direction except the way we wanted to travel—north-east. Finally it terminated in a road that ran east and west. Taking an eastern direction, we came to a small village. In trying to circle around it, we ran into a wagon-maker's shop. It was quite dark, for the moon had not risen yet; we tried to find a road that would take us north-east; we found one that ran north, and followed it for several miles, when it turned south, and intersected the old road again. At last we found a road that took us north-east, through a rich country, and by the light of the moon, which now shone nearly as bright as day, we could see the country for miles. We continued our journey until near morning before we halted; distance, twenty miles.

At daylight, August 24th, we found ourselves in an exposed position. We therefore hid in a large green tree-top, that was lying on the ground near by, and went to sleep again. Just as the sun rose, Lieut. Srofe awoke me, saying: "The hounds are on our track again!" On, on they came, yelping and howling as on a former occasion. They were too close on us to attempt to get away from them this time, and what made the matter worse, there were no small trees close by to climb, out of their reach, so we laid still, awaiting our fate.

When the hounds got opposite us, instead of turning off into the woods from the road, as we had done, they kept straight ahead. It was quite evident after they had passed us, that they were off our track. They now quit barking, but kept running around in every direction. Presently two men on horseback came up, blowing their hunter's horns and urging up the dogs. When we saw them pass by, we took courage and started off in an opposite direction as fast as we could run. We had, however, proceeded but a short distance, when we heard them coming after us, with the old yelp. It now became an exciting race, and our re-capture seemed to be only a question of time. Rubbing soap on the bottom of our shoes did excellent service again, in breaking the scent of the hounds. Whenever we reached a stream we dashed into the water, and followed its course for a considerable distance, for the purpose of misleading the dogs. Twice we were about to give ourselves up, but each time, after taking a short rest, we started off to try it once more. For the third time we halted. Panting, and almost out of breath, we stood by the small trees that we had selected to climb, out of reach of the hounds. Our preparations to surrender were completed, and the hounds were gaining on us fast, when I asked Lieut. Srofe the question: "Camp Ford, or Little Rock?" His answer came quick, "Little Rock!" and grasping his haversack, he started at the top of his speed, and I followed after.

It was nearly noon when we struck a bayou. We found a shallow place and waded to the opposite shore. After we had crossed, we felt secure, with such a large body of water between us and our pursuers, and our trail obliterated where we entered the bayou. They now began to lose ground, and finally the baying of the hounds ceased altogether. Being very hungry, and nearly run down, we selected the first favorable locality, built a fire, and parched some corn. While thus busily engaged, we heard some persons approaching and talking very loud. We had no more than put out our fire and hid ourselves, when two men passed near by, without, however, discovering us. A short time afterwards, a hunting party returned to the prison, and reported that they had killed a Yankee Major and a Lieutenant, across the Sabine river!

We started again at dark and followed the road for a few hours, when it entered a very dark and gloomy-looking swamp. We could only keep in the road by following the wagon-ruts. Finally, the road terminated at a small patch of corn, in a clearing, in the midst of a heavy-timbered bottom. We groped around on our hands and knees, trying to find a road that would take us farther, but all in vain. At last we decided to lay down and snatch a few hours sleep until the moon rose. We awoke when the moon was about half an hour high. It was now light, compared to what it had been, but still we could find no road that would take us any farther. We then retraced our steps, and soon struck a road that we had missed before, which took us north-east. We knew now that we were nearing a large stream, from the quantity of water around us. Near daylight we found that we were correct. The stream proved to be Little Cypress River, distance twenty miles.

CHAPTER II.

Making a Raft — Crossing Little Cypress — Wading the Overflowed Bottoms — Crossing Big Cypress — Crossing Sulphur Fork — Wading and Swimming — Pass for a Rebel Deserter — Begging for Something to Eat — Relating Camp Rumors — Journey Interrupted by Rain — Capturing a Slave on a Mule — In the Indian Territory — Out of Our Course — Conversation with Three Slaves — The First Dinner — Carried Down the Stream — A Night Among the Owls and Mosquitos — Fording Little River.

AUGUST 25th, made a raft and crossed at sunrise. The raft was made by tying two logs together with grape-vines, then we made a platform of short pieces of wood, on which we tied our clothes, rations, matches, etc., and swimming alongside, pushed it across the stream. During the day we saw a man chopping wood, but fortunately were not seen by him. In the afternoon we traveled through woods, covered with small mounds, and saw quite a number of deer of all sizes. We had thought of resting all night, but toward evening a small boy passed us on horseback, in consequence of which we traveled until near morning. Distance, twenty-five miles.

August 26th, at daylight, we pursued our journey, and traveled through an almost impenetrable Texas chapparal. We found some splendid grapes, which partly paid us for our torn clothes. At about 8 o'clock A. M. we came to a bottom covered with water, through which we waded for about a mile, when we reached the banks of Big Cypress. The heavy rains up the river, the week previous, had overflowed all the river bottoms. We made a raft and crossed at 9 o'clock A. M. and found plenty of grapes on the opposite shore. We rested during the middle of the day, and parched more corn.

We had not traveled far, after we resumed our journey, until we struck another bottom, covered waist-deep with water, which gave evidence of another stream ahead. After wading in a short distance, we were compelled to turn back, the water being too deep to wade. We then retraced our steps and followed the base of the hills to the north, in search of a better place to reach the banks of the stream. After traveling a few hours, we were so fortunate as to find dry ground leading to the river. It proved to be Sulphur Fork of Red River, which was wider than any stream we had crossed before. We made a raft and crossed it about 4 o'clock P. M.

When we reached the opposite side, we could scarcely find a dry place to land, all the surrounding bottoms being covered with water. While going through the cane-brake, we had to part the cane with our hands, and then crowd ourselves through as best we could, the water, most of the time, being waist-deep. On we dragged our weary limbs, until we came to a deep place, where we had to swim, by way of change. The sun was sinking in the west, but we were still wading through water, mud and mire, with no better prospect of a dry bed for the night than to climb a tree, and wait for the coming day.

The sun had set, and night was fast approaching, when we struck the upland, having traveled a distance of twenty-three miles that day. I will not attempt to describe our feelings when we stepped from the water to dry land. Suffice it to say, that we did not travel far until we laid down for the night and slept soundly, considering that our clothing was thoroughly saturated with water.

August 27th, we awoke in the morning, stiff and sore, which wore off as we traveled on. We saw a woman going through the woods, but were not seen by her. This proved to be the hottest day of our trip, and we had less protection from the scorching sun, as the country was almost destitute of timber. In the afternoon we struck the sand-barrens, which were entirely destitute of water to drink. We were so overcome by the heat and thirst, that we were unable to proceed on our journey. On examining our canteens, we found that we had one pint of water left, which we shared equally, and concealed ourselves in the undergrowth for the rest of the day.

Toward evening, the want of water drove us from our resting-place. We determined now, at all hazards, to follow the first bed of a stream until we found water to allay our burning thirst. We soon struck the bed of quite a large creek, but no water. It was completely dried up. We followed its windings until near midnight, when we found a small stagnant pool in the bed of the stream. Here we halted and drank to our heart's content, and for fear we might suffer for water during the night, we concluded to remain there until morning, having traveled about sixteen miles that day.

August 28th. This was the ninth day out; and we supposed that we were about one hundred and fifty miles north-east from Camp Ford, but were not certain, as we had not spoken to any one since we left the stockade. We had our maps ready for reference, if we could only find out the name of any town near us. To learn that, I agreed to stop at the first house, and inquire of the slaves what neighborhood we were in. At ten o'clock A. M., we came to a house in the woods, and I saw some persons that I took to be slaves, but found out afterwards that I was mistaken.

I had settled the matter in my mind how I would talk to them, but had not calculated on meeting white people. We were well aware that we could rely on the blacks for assistance, but had to give the whites as wide a berth as possible. But, to be prepared for any emergency, I went north of the house, and passed by to the south, as though I was going to Texas instead of north. Just as I came in sight of the house, I saw two white men and several women and children, sitting at the door. They saw me before I did them, so there was no alternative but to stop and get out of the difficulty the best way I could. This was something I was not prepared for, and there was no time to lose in inventing some plausible story, as the house was not more than fifty yards distant.

As I approached to where they were sitting, I began to fan myself vigorously with my old straw hat. The perspiration was oozing out at every pore, from mere excitement. I bid them the time of day, which they returned, and invited me to take a seat. I made a few trifling remarks about the weather; they, however, did not seem to pay much attention to what I said, but stared at me in a manner which seemed to say: "Well, who are you?" Finally a perfect silence prevailed. I was still fanning, and they were staring. The suspense and silence began to make me nervous, so I thought, "now or never."

I commenced by asking: "How far is it to Washington?" I thought there was a town in that vicinity by that name. One of them replied: "It is about thirteen miles down to Washington." I knew from my map where I was, so I began to have more confidence. I then told them that I belonged to a Texas regiment, at Arkadelphia, Arkansas, and that my mother, who lived in Henderson, Texas, and was a widow, had sent for me to come home on business, and that as I could not

get a furlough, I had determined to go home on
my own responsibility, attend to my affairs, and
then return to my regiment. If they wished, they
could have me arrested as a deserter, and sent
back, but I would get home some time. Besides,
my captain told me that if I hurried back, there
would be nothing said about it. I awaited anx-
iously to see what effect my story would have on
them. It seemed to take very well. One remarked that I was rather bold about it. The other said
they were not near as hard on deserters as they
used to be, and I thought from his looks that he
spoke from personal experience.

They now asked me the news in camp. I made
up a batch of stories for the occasion, but told
them they were mere camp rumors, and that you
could not believe anything you heard these days.
I then said I would like to have something to eat.
The old man said he did not know about that. If
his neighbors knew that he was harboring deserters, it would go hard with him. I had no more
than made the request, when the lady of the house,
a middle-aged woman, with a remarkably large
group of children around her, started out the back-
way, and soon returned with a loaf of corn bread,
and a large tin of buttermilk. As soon as it was
handed to me, I began to demolish the corn-bread,
and looking up, saw the whole crowd staring at
me in silence. I felt embarrassed, and feared that
they suspected I was an escaped Union prisoner.
The only thing suspicious about my conversation

was, that when I was asked when I left Arkadelphia, I replied, "the day before yesterday." I found out afterwards, that we were one hundred miles from that place. I concluded that I had better be going, and remarked that I wanted to be traveling before it got much hotter, and requested them to point out the direction I should take to go to Washington. The old man went so far as to go part of the way into the woods, to put me on the right course. I went in the given direction until I got out of his sight, then circled round to where Lieut. Srofe was hid in a brush-heap, awaiting my return. In a few words, I told him what I had seen and heard. We hastily examined our maps, and found the exact locality we were in. We had kept our general course well, and had traveled 157 miles since we left the prison.

We now concluded to make very fast time, and get out of that neighborhood, to keep out of the way of the hounds. We had not proceeded very far when it began to cloud up, and soon the rain came pattering down upon us. With the sun hidden from our view, we could not travel to any purpose, so we sat down on a log, with our coats thrown over our heads, and took the rain from about noon until nearly dark, without any intermission. As soon as it had ceased raining, we built a shelter of pine boughs, and then a fire, parched corn, and put up for the night. Distance traveled, fourteen miles.

The following morning, August 29th, we discovered a log cabin within sight of our shelter, therefore we made haste to get out of that vicinity. After traveling several hours, we crossed an unfinished railroad track, and soon after reached the Red River. We made a raft, and crossed at 8 o'clock, A. M. On reaching the opposite shore, we found a swamp, covered with a rank undergrowth of every description, but we made every effort to get out on the upland as soon as possible. After creeping through cane-brakes, briars, vines and burs, for about an hour and a half, we struck the same river again that we had crossed. We followed the river to the north, until it made a direct turn to the west; we then turned off to the east, through a dense cane-brake, to make sure of leaving the stream behind us, and striking the upland. In about one hour's travel we came to the same river once more, near a house, situated on the bank of the stream. This was rather discouraging. It was now near noon, and we had crossed the river at 8 o'clock that morning, and had traveled ever since without resting, and yet had made no progress. It was evident now that we were lost in the river bottoms, and in the windings of the stream could not find our way out. We, however, took our north-east course once more by the sun, and passed through an extensive swamp, terminating at last in a comparatively large lake. After crossing this with some difficulty, we found ourselves in an open country. At about 2 o'clock P. M., we halted to rest and dry our provisions, at the same time hiding under a thicket of Osage Orange.

We supposed that here we would be safe from all intrusion, but we had scarcely laid down when we heard some one approaching us. Nearer and nearer he came; we could not run, not knowing what direction to take to get away from the threatened danger. I raised up, and began to look around cautiously, when I saw a negro on a mule, coming directly toward us. I crawled up in the bushes to where I thought he would have to pass, then, as soon as he came within my reach, I ordered him to halt. At the same time I caught his mule by the bridle. The slave was so scared at my sudden appearance that he trembled from head to foot, and could not answer my questions for some time. I asked him the name of the nearest town; he said he did not know, and did not know the name of any town anywhere. I then asked him how far around there he was acquainted; he replied, "about ten miles."

There was a poor prospect of finding out our whereabouts from him. After telling him we were runaway Yankees, and making him promise that he would not tell any person that he had seen us, I was about to let him go, when I asked him where he lived. He said, "about three miles on the State Line road." I asked him, "what State Line?" He replied, "Between Arkansas and the Indian Territory." We knew, then, exactly what locality we were in. We had missed our course by going too far west, and had strayed over into the Choctaw Reservation. Before he left he warned us not to go too far to our left, because there were a lot of soldiers over there.

After we had gained all the information we could from him, we let him go. When we found we were out of our course, we did not tarry long to rest, but started off due east. Towards evening, we ran against ten or fifteen slaves in a field, gathering corn. We turned back into the woods, and tried to circle around the plantation, by keeping in the timber; but we had to give up that plan, as we could see the cleared land on either side of us for miles; therefore our only chance was to cross the fields, in sight of the dwelling-houses on our right and left. We succeeded in creeping along the fence and through the weeds, into the woods on the opposite side, without being seen. We traveled until nine o' clock that night, and then rested until morning, having traveled that day a distance of eighteen miles.

August 30th, we started at daylight and had traveled but a short distance, when it began to cloud up, with strong indications of rain. As we could not keep in our course without seeing the sun, we waited until noon, when it cleared off. At the first glimpse of the sun, we started on our journey. After traveling a short time, we came across a lot of green timber, that evidently had been cut down that day, and on looking around, saw three slaves watching us, not more than a hundred yards off. We concluded that the best plan would be to go and tell them who we were, and caution them against telling any one that they had seen us. On asking them the name of the nearest town, we were told that they lived in Rocky Comfort, Arkansas, which was four miles west from there. They also gave us the cheering information that four runaway Yankees had been caught in that neighborhood the week previous. We asked them if they could give us something to eat. They examined their dinner-basket, and found that there was about a pound of bacon and a piece of corn-bread left, which they gave us. We divided it equally, and inmediately commenced devouring the fat bacon, while the slaves looked on in amazement.

After making them promise not to mention having seen us, we pursued our journey. About an hour afterwards, we came near running against an old man on horseback, before we saw him. All that we could do was to drop flat on the bare ground, there being no brush of any kind near. We were in great danger of being seen, but although he passed very near us, he did not look in our direction. He appeared to be in a deep study, neither looking to the right nor left.

We struck a road towards evening, and rested until night, then followed it through a large plantation, which we entered through a gate, swung across the road. About ten o'clock that night, we came to a small, but very rapid stream. I waded into the water, but found it too deep and swift to cross at that point, and in trying to get back to the bank, the force of the stream carried me down into the swift, foamy current. After some difficulty, I managed to get on shore. In the second attempt, we crossed without any further mishap.

The road, which seemed much lower than its surroundings, now wound through a dark and dreary swamp, covered with water, which made traveling disagreeable and tiresome. When splashing through the water, we knew that we were in the road; when we struck dry land we knew that we were off the track; therefore had to search for the water again. We traveled on until near morning—longer than we wished to, but we were anxious to strike the upland before we halted, and get out of the water and away from the millions of mosquitos; but we could not accomplish impossibilities, and were obliged to drop down by the road-side, to await the coming day.

To sleep was out of the question, with the mosquitos innumerable and as ravenous as wolves, while the frogs and owls were making night hideous with their cries. To protect us from the mosquitos, we gathered a large pile of pine boughs, then crawled underneath them, to await the coming morning. The memory of that night's suffering, I will never forget. Distance traveled, eighteen miles.

August 31st, at the first signs of day, we were up and gone. In a short time we saw a house, where a woman stood at the gate, calling up the hogs, but we passed around to the rear of the building without being seen. We crossed a dense swamp, and forded Little River in the forenoon. We traveled until about nine o'clock that night, when we entered another swamp, covered with water, similar to the one we had passed through the evening before. Finding too much water ahead, we turned back, picked out a dry spot, and put up for the night. Distance that day, twenty-three miles.

CHAPTER III.

RE-CAPTURED.

The Arkansas Hills—The Hum of the Spinning-Wheel—
The Last Match—Roast Pumpkin and Parched Corn—
Almost Home—Re-Captured—Bound With Ropes—
A Retrograde Movement—Another Unfortunate Yan-
kee—On Exhibition—Entertained by Young Ladies—
The Old Lady's Lecture on the War—Sent to Wash-
ington, Arkansas—The Guests in the Parlor—In the
Court House—Offer of "Jewelry"—Rebel Officers on a
Spree—On the Road to Camden—Battle-Field of Prairie
d' Ann—Eating Two Days' Rations for Supper—Slaugh-
ter of the Colored Troops—No Quarter.

SEPTEMBER 1st. We started at daybreak, and made another attempt to get through the swamp before us. After a two hours' tramp we reached cleared land, and found plenty of grapes and muscadines. We forded a stream at about 8 o'clock, A. M., and reached the Arkansas hills about an hour afterward. In traveling through the woods we could hear the hum of the spinning-wheel, at intervals, on all sides, which enabled us to give the houses on our route as wide a berth as necessary. That day we heard more of them than usual, on account of the country being more thickly settled.

About noon, we halted at a small creek, near a

corn-field. By referring to our maps, we found we were 225 miles from the prison, and about 75 miles from Little Rock, Arkansas. Lieut. Srofe made a fire with the last match, while I procured some corn from an adjoining field, of which we parched a sufficient quantity to last us until we would reach our lines, which we thought, if nothing happened, would take us between three and four days. Feeling confident of success, we even talked of what we would eat and drink when we got through, and the good times we were going to have generally. We were also going to do all we could to have the poor fellows released, whom we had left in Texas. But such is the uncertainty of human calculations.

After we had finished parching corn, we attempted to eat a roasted pumpkin, in which, hungry as we were, we failed. We now pursued our journey once more, in high spirits, and traveled far into the night before we halted, a distance, in all, of twenty-three miles.

September 2d, we were on the road bright and early, and halted at a cool spring at 7 o'clock A. M. We, however, did not tarry long, being now in a hurry to get home. An hour afterward, while traveling through the woods, we discovered a road ahead of us, which crossed our route. We were about fifty yards from it, when we halted to listen. Hearing a wagon coming on our left, we held a hurried consultation, whether to attempt to cross the road before the wagon came in sight, or to run back and hide in the underbrush until it had passed by. Knowing that we could not cross the road without being seen, we ran back a short distance and hid in the brush.

The wagon came rumbling along slowly, and when opposite us I looked up cautiously, and saw two men in it, busily engaged in conversation, and slashing the whip at the oxen they were driving. I was convinced that they had not seen us, so I laid down again to wait until they were out of sight, before we would venture any farther. They had passed but a short distance, however, when they halted. We thought they might have broken something about their wagon, and had stopped to repair it. They were still talking very loud, when we heard some one approaching through the brush toward us. I began to feel uneasy, and raised up cautiously to see what was going on. As I looked up, I saw a rebel on a mule, with his gun pointed toward us, not more than thirty yards off. At the same time he ordered us to " come out o' thar ! " Had a thunderbolt from a clear sky descended in our midst, it could not have dumbfounded us more completely. In the meantime the rebel had lowered his gun; but as we did not stir, he raised it once more, and again ordered us to " come out o' thar !" I requested him not to shoot—that we would surrender. He then ordered us to march to the wagon, where the two men were awaiting our arrival.

My first question to them was, " how did you happen to see us when you passed by ?" The rebel on the mule, overhearing my question, replied, that the two men in the wagon did not see us, but that he had been on picket, and was just going home from the opposite direction, when he saw us come near the road, and watched us until we ran back and hid in the brush. We were so taken up with the wagon, that we did not think of looking to our right, where the rebel, not a hundred yards distant, was a silent spectator of the whole proceeding. He heard the rumbling of the wagon at the same time we did, and concluded to wait until it came up, and get assistance to capture us.

In reply to their questions, we informed them who we were, and where we came from, but they did not seem to believe our statement, and searched us to see whether we had any weapons concealed about our persons; but they found nothing more than an old case-knife. They then tied our arms behind our backs with ropes, and with another rope tied us together. The rebel on the mule then took charge of us, and said he was going to take us to Lieut. Shote's house, about seven miles from there, and the men with the wagon continued their journey in the opposite direction.

This was all done so suddenly, that it seemed like a dream to me, and more than once I found myself, as I have often done when dreaming a horrible dream, trying to arouse myself, to find it all an illusion; but this time it was impossible—the stern reality was before me. The excitement that had kept me up so far was now over; I felt weak and hungry, and begged our captor for something to eat. The first house we came to we halted, and the guard procured us some corn-bread, then took us to a blacksmith's shop, near by, and partially loosened the ropes with which we were bound, while he and the blacksmith kept a vigilant watch over us. After we had eaten our corn-bread, the ropes were re-adjusted, and we resumed our journey.

It must have been seven very long miles that he marched us, as we did not reach the Lieutenant's house until the middle of the afternoon. The house was situated in the midst of a dense pine forest, with no cleared land around it. As we stepped into the house, some one said in a loud voice, addressing my partner: "How are you, Srofe?" I was astonished, and Lieut. Srofe did not understand it either. I looked around the room, and saw a young man, dressed in the rebel gray, lying on the floor, reading a book. I asked him who he was, and where he came from. He replied that his name was John Baker, and that he belonged to the 130th regiment Illinois Infantry, and had made his escape from Camp Ford, Texas, but was recaptured about an hour before. Miserable as we felt, we had a good laugh over our meeting. This convinced the rebels that we were Yankees, and no mistake.

His story was soon told. He had bribed the guards and made his escape with the others the evening before we did, but became separated from them, and had made the trip alone. That morning he ran against this house in the woods, and was confronted by the inmates before he was aware of it. Being confused, he could only stammer out, " How far is it to Little Rock? "—just the very question he should not have asked. The Lieutenant, who was in the house, overheard him, and came to the door, his hand resting on his revolver, told him to walk in and make himself comfortable, which he did, saying that he was beaten this time. Hence our strange meeting. This same soldier made his escape at two different times afterwards; was re-captured each time, and the close of the war found him still in prison.

But to resume our own adventures. The rebel Lieutenant had us untied, and gave us our dinners, after which a wounded Confederate soldier, from Lee's army, who had just returned home on furlough, entertained us with an account of the military operations east of the Mississippi River. Towards evening, we were put in charge of four or five rebel guards, who took us about six miles farther, to Serg't. Luther's house, to stay all night. They had now three live Yankees, as they called us, to exhibit around through the country. They took great pride in showing their prize to all their friends on the road, but we were a hard-looking set to exhibit.

Our clothes were all in shreds, from traveling so long through the brush, and not very clean, at that. We were considered quite a curiosity wherever we were taken. At one place the guards halted us at a house to get some water, and told the family to come and see their live Yankees. They came out, expecting to see a great sight, no doubt. An old lady, in particular, ran back into the house, and returned with her spectacles, which she hastily, in her excitement, pushed up on her forehead, and then planted herself right before us, and took a good look. After she had gazed at us in silence for some time, she exclaimed: "Well, if these be Yankees, they look almost like we 'uns." It is very strange what queer ideas some of the Southern people had, in regard to the appearance of Northern soldiers.

About dusk that evening, we reached the log cabin of Serg't. Luther, where they intended to keep us for the night. The family consisted of the mother and her two young daughters. Serg't. Luther had taken some deserters to a neighboring town that day, and had not yet returned. They prepared supper for us, consisting of green beans, pork and corn-bread, which we ate by the light of a pine torch. After supper, the ladies entertained us by singing some songs of *"Ante Bellum"* days. Their favorite seemed to be the "Bold Buccaneer."

After they got through, they requested us to teach them some new ones, but as we were not on a singing excursion, we respectfully declined. The fact of the case was, we had not learned many new songs since the war, excepting such as "John Brown," "Rally Round the Flag," and that style of patriotic airs, which we were not very anxious to sing in the presence of so many armed rebels. Not knowing what disposition they were going to make of us for the night, we informed them that we were very tired and sleepy. The old lady then made a bed on the floor, in the only room the cabin contained, while she and her daughters occupied the beds, and the guards, with loaded muskets, stood at the doors.

Before the old lady retired, she gave us a bit of her mind. She inquired: "How much longer is this war going to last?" To which we replied, that we did not know. She said: "Dog my cats, I think it has been going on long enough, and this thing of the women having to raise the 'craps,' while the men are riding around the whole year, with their guns, will have to be stopped mighty soon. I am getting tired of doing all the work." We half-way agreed with her, but were too tired and sleepy to stay awake and listen to the lecture, and fell into a sound slumber while she was yet talking.

Up to this time, according to our maps, we had traveled two hundred and fifty-three miles. The air-line was two hundred and twenty-five miles from prison, thirty miles west of Hot Springs, and eighty miles from Little Rock, Arkansas. To have all our trials and sufferings terminate thus, with perhaps still worse in store, made our future look very gloomy and discouraging.

Sept. 3d, long before day, the guards awakened

us, saying that we must get ready to march, and we would eat our breakfast on the road. Their orders were to take us to Washington, Ark., 45 miles south, and turn us over to the authorities there. Towards evening, the guards requested, at each house on the road, permission to stay all night, and get supper for themselves and prisoners, and feed for their horses, but at every house the reply came, "we have nothing to eat ourselves."

It was getting dark, and we had marched 27 miles since morning, when we halted at the house of a wealthy planter, near Center Point, but he turned them off with the same answer they had received elsewhere. We then begged the guards not to march us any farther, telling them we would be perfectly satisfied with a little parched corn, if they would only stop for the night. After a short consultation among the guards, they entered the house, which was a large brick mansion, and took forcible possession of the premises, and ordered supper for the guards and prisoners, which was served up with reluctance. After supper, we were put in the parlor, with a sentinel stationed at the door.

The next day, we passed through Temperanceville and Nashville, and reached Washington in the evening. Here we were confined in the second story of the Court House. The next morning, a rebel officer called on us, and, after inquiring who we were, asked me whether I was fond of jewelry. I replied, "I don't know that I am, particularly."

He said he would procure some for us before night. I did not then comprehend him, but learned afterward, that he intended to give us a ball and chain to carry. They had sent off some Union prisoners a few days previous, who carried off all the shackles and chains in the town, which was all that saved us.

The day following, a rebel Colonel, from Missouri, paid us a visit. He treated us very gentlemanly, and took out his pocket-book and asked us whether we wanted any money. We thanked him, but declined. He then asked us whether he could do anything for us. We replied that all we wanted was to be sent back to our old prison, as soon as possible, so that we would be in time for an exchange, if any took place. He said he would send us forward as soon as he could get the guards ready, which would be three or four days. At the same time, he remarked that there was then an exchange of prisoners taking place at our old prison, and that we would have to hurry up to be in time. We were all excitement now, to get back to Camp Ford, for we had strong hopes of being exchanged if we arrived before it took place. That day three more Union prisoners, belonging to an Indiana regiment, were brought in. One of the poor fellows died, a few days afterward, from the exposure of the trip.

September 8th. This was the day set for us to be sent to Camden, Arkansas, sixty miles distant. Early in the morning, several rebel officers from

Missouri, with whom we had become acquainted, came and took Lieut. Srofe and myself out of the guard-house, to show us the town and give us our breakfast. Washington was then the capital of Arkansas, and all the rebel work-shops for the State were located there. After a walk through the town, we visited a saloon, where all they had was very mean " pine-top " whisky, at one dollar a drink. The rebel officers, excepting one, got most gloriously drunk in a very short time. In our army, the rule among the great drinkers seemed to be, to get drunk only when in good spirits, after a victory. We had nothing to rejoice over, therefore, I am happy to say, we did not follow their example, but reminded them that we had not had our breakfast. They then took us to their quarters, where breakfast was waiting, consisting of fried beef liver, very sad-looking biscuits, and corn coffee. We cleared the table of everything within our reach, in a remarkably short time.

The rebels were getting boisterous, declaring that they were going to fight us as long as they lived, to gain their independence, and said that what we saw on the table was their regular fare, but they would live on sweet potatoes, before they would give up. We were not in a fighting condition just then, therefore let them have it all their own way.

At 11 o'clock A. M., we, with three other Union prisoners and several rebel deserters, were turned over to a squad of rebel cavalry, under Lieutenant

Whitehouse. We had to march thirty miles a day, but otherwise we received fair treatment from them. We traveled over the same road that Gen. Steele had fought the rebels on, the previous spring. The marks of the fierce conflict that raged over that narrow country road, were still visible on all sides. In the afternoon we crossed the battlefield of Prairie d' Ann, and reached the home of Lieutenant Whitehouse in the evening. For safe keeping, we were placed in the village store, and received rations to last us two days, which we cooked and ate during the night, from the effects of which I felt very uncomfortable all the next day. Two days Confederate rations of corn-meal and bacon, was more than I could stand at one meal.

We made an early start the following morning, and soon reached Poison Springs, where a portion of Gen. Steele's supply train had been captured by the rebels. Among the train-guards was a regiment of colored soldiers, five hundred strong. They were surrounded by the rebels, no quarter given, and every one killed. Their bodies were still lying where they fell, and their bones scattered along the road. A Southern historian mentions the slaughter of the colored regiment, and states that "among the material fruits of the battle, was an uncounted number of dead negroes."

CHAPTER IV.

In the Cotton-Shed at Camden—Pandemonium—Sent to the Hospital—On the Road Again—Guarded by Blood-Hounds—Prisoners Lassoed—Wading Through a Stream by Request—Arrival at Shreveport—Meeting Our Regiment—Homeward Bound—Our First Mail—No Water for " Yankees "—Camp Ford—Home Again—Sentenced —Our New Cabin—Northers—Presidential Election— Tramping in the Ring.

SEPTEMBER 10th, we arrived at Camden, traveling the entire distance, sixty miles, in forty-eight hours. Here we were turned over to one of the meanest men in existence, whose name has slipped my memory. He was a Captain and Prison-Adjutant. Although he did not misuse me individually, I have seen him vent his spleen on more than one poor fellow. His chief amusement consisted in flogging slaves, who were found away from home without passes, putting Union soldiers in the stocks, or chaining them together in pairs, and making them work on the corduroy roads, near town. After he had taken our names, he put us in the second story of a long and very narrow ware-house, with only two windows at each end, for ventilation, in which were confined between two and three hundred prisoners. Quite a number of them had also been re-captured in attempting to make their escape.

That night I could hardly find sufficient space on the floor to lie down, the room being so crowded, and the heat so oppressive that it was impossible to sleep. The next day they took all the worst men of their own army, whom they had confined for various offenses in the neighboring guard-houses, together with the Union prisoners and quite a number of slaves, that had attempted to escape from their masters, and put us all in a cotton-shed.

It was a low building, and occupied nearly an entire square, with a hollow court in the center. This was decidedly a hard place, as hot as an oven, with next to nothing to eat, and a very scanty allowance of warm river-water to drink. In the center of the shed, the cooking was done for all the inmates. We had but very few cooking utensils, therefore those who did not get to cook their rations by daylight, had to keep up the fires and do their cooking after nightfall. About one-fourth of the prisoners had a ball and chain to their legs, or were chained together in pairs. To awake during the night, and hear the yelling and cursing, the rattling of chains, and see the air filled with sparks and ashes, as the fires were stirred up by the cooks, was enough to make one believe that he was in Pandemonium.

With insufficient food, bad weather, and worn out from traveling so far, I was afraid it would bring on sickness, which, in such a place, would be equal to a through ticket to eternity. I learned from the guards, that there was a Union hospital in town, containing several hundred wounded soldiers, that had been captured from Gen. Steele's command, in charge of two of our own Doctors. We managed to send a note out to the Surgeon in charge, telling him how we were situated; that we had no clothes fit to wear, and scarcely anything to eat. He sent us word to keep quiet; that he would have us paroled and sent to his hospital. Among other articles sent through the lines by our Government, for the use of the wounded, was a barrel of whisky. By using it occasionally among the officers in charge of us, he gained their consent to have Lieut. Srofe and myself paroled, and sent to the hospital.

When we reached the hospital, we thought our happiness was complete, we were so kindly greeted by all. We both received a suit of army blue, and plenty to eat. Here we met Maj. McCauley and his comrade, of whose capture, near Rock Comfort, Arkansas, the three slaves had previously informed us.

September 30th, all the Union prisoners that were able to travel, numbering about three hundred, were ordered to Shreveport, Louisiana, one hundred and ten miles distant. We were guarded by a company of cavalry, in command of Captain Montgomery, whose very name was a terror to the Union prisoners. I had heard of his brutal treatment of Federal soldiers, and was continually on my guard, not to incur his displeasure. Behind the last file of prisoners rode five rebels, with lariats, with orders to lasso and drag every one by the neck that did not keep up with the cavalry guards.

Many a poor fellow was thus terribly punished for failing to keep ahead of the "ropers," as they were called. One young soldier was lassoed so often, and failing to travel with the rope around his neck, as fast as the mounted "ropers," he was dragged so frequently that he died from the effects of it, about a week after he reached Camp Ford. Capt. Franz, of the 9th Wisconsin Vols., whose arm had been amputated but a short time previous, and who was still suffering from the effects of the operation, was unable to keep up one day. He was told by the "ropers" that, unless he marched faster, they would put the rope around his neck. He halted where he stood, and replied, that he was marching as fast as he could, and that they were welcome to do their worst—he could do no better. They made no reply, nor did they molest him after that. Capt. Franz informed me afterward, that he felt so miserable, that had they taken his life on the spot he would have considered it a deed of mercy.

Behind the "ropers" were another set of tormentors, consisting of three rebels, with a pack of blood-hounds, to hunt down those who attempted to escape. It was almost impossible to get away from them, and yet two of our men were so foolhardy as to make the attempt. As soon as they were missed, the rebels put the hounds on their trail, and in the course of four or five hours afterward the rebels, with the dogs, caught up with us again. When asked by their comrades whether they had caught the " Yankees," they replied that the dogs had killed one of them before they came up, and the other was so badly torn that they had to leave him in a hospital on the road ! That was the last I ever heard of either of them.

When we halted for the night, after the first day's march from Camden, Capt. Montgomery laid out our camping-ground by driving stakes at the four corners. One of the prisoners, not knowing how the stakes came there, pulled one of them up to kindle a fire with. The Captain saw him in the act, and came rushing up, took the stake out of his hand, and without saying a word, struck him on the head with it and felled him to the ground.

It rained nearly all night, and as we had no protection from the weather, we spent a miserable night. The next morning it was very muddy traveling, and the small streams on the road were out of their banks. In trying to avoid wading through the water of a small stream, by crossing on a foot-log by the road-side, a guard called me back, after I was half-way across, and ordered me to wade through the water in the middle of the road; at the same time he halted his horse and aimed his gun at me. Consequently, I hurried back and floundered through the water, to his entire satisfaction. This is a fair specimen of our treatment while on the road to the stockade.

We arrived at Shreveport on the 5th of October, having marched one hundred and ten miles in four days and a half. Shreveport was the headquarters of the rebel army, west of the Mississippi River. I counted eight steamboats and two gunboats at the wharf, and the streets were crowded with rebel soldiers.

We crossed Red River on a pontoon bridge, in front of the city, and marched up Main Street to the Provost Marshal's office. While our names were being taken by that officer, Capt. Birchett, the rebel Assistant Agent for the Exchange of Prisoners, with whom I was well acquainted, came walking along the side-walk. As soon as he saw me, he stepped up to where I stood, and said, "Where in the world did you come from?" I replied that I had made my escape, but had been re-captured in Arkansas. He said, "you missed it this time, sure; your regiment has just arrived at the Four Mile Springs, paroled, and are on their way home." I had never thought of an exchange taking place so soon. I tried to smile and pretend I did not care, but I think I made a failure of it. He stepped back and began talking with the rebels who crowded around him, and from the manner in which they stared at me, I supposed he was giving them my history.

From there they took us about two miles out of town, to a rebel camp. Here we remained four days, and during that time they kept telling us that we would be sent home with our Regiment, which was as hard a punishment as they could have inflicted, as it raised our hopes of release, only to disappoint them.

On the 8th day of October, we were ordered to start immediately for Camp Ford, 110 miles west. We were still guarded by the same cavalry, and in the same manner as before. A few hours march brought us to where our Regiment was encamped by the roadside, waiting for the rebels to repair their steamboats, to take them to the Mississippi River. They had heard that Lieut. Srofe and myself were on our way back to prison, and had collected all the spare change in the Regiment, which amounted to twenty dollars in green-backs and two dollars in silver. As we passed by, Capt. Thomas Montgomery, of my Regiment, gave the money, and the letters that had arrived for us during our absence, to one of the guards, who handed them over to me. In a few words I gave Capt. Montgomery instructions what to do with my private property that had not been captured, and to do all he could to have us exchanged. The paroled prisoners had received strict orders, that if any one of them conversed with us as we passed, they would be sent back again to the stockade; consequently, the conversation was necessarily carried on entirely by myself.

All the hardships and suffering of my three years' service seemed to dwindle into insignificance when compared to the utter despair I felt on that memorable day; and it was with a heavy heart and weary footsteps that I resumed my westward journey after my brief interview.

The incidents of the march, the perusal of the first letters received since my capture, in which I received the first intimation that I had been reported among the killed, in the official report of the battle of Sabine Cross-Roads, and that little word, "Hope," all tended toward wearing off the first disappointment, at missing my chance of exchange with my Regiment. After a tiresome march of twenty-five miles, we camped in the evening near a deserted cavalry camp, where I found a lot of corn-cobs, with a few grains of corn at each end, which the horses had not eaten off. I began to gather them up, and had quite an arm-full, when a rebel seeing me, asked what I intended to do with those cobs. I replied that I was going to parch the corn for my supper. He seemed surprised, and told me to throw it away and he would get me some good corn. That evening he brought me four large ears, which I was almost tempted to keep for myself, but upon second thought, I divided it equally with my messmates.

The pint of corn-meal, and the small slice of bacon, that we received daily, was insufficient food on which to march from 25 to 30 miles a day, and but for stray ears of corn that we picked up on the march, and the few crumbs begged of the guards, some of the prisoners would never have reached the stockade.

The next morning, when Lieut. Srofe awoke, he discovered that one of the rebels had stolen his blouse while he was asleep. He found the soldier that had taken it, but no amount of persuasion could induce him to return it to the rightful owner. Lieut. Srofe then delivered a free lecture on stealing, for the benefit of the guards. As the blouse was not returned, Lieut. Srofe resumed the journey in his shirt-sleeves.

That evening we camped near a rebel's house, who refused to let "Yankees" have any water from his well, without which we could not prepare our corn-meal. After trying in vain to eat it raw, we parched it slightly, which made it more palatable. Some time in the night the guards discovered some stagnant pools of water near camp, which they permitted us to use.

October 12th, we arrived at Camp Ford, Texas, our old home. We had marched the distance from Shreveport, one hundred and ten miles, in four days. After calling the roll, we were turned over to the prison-commander, Col. Brown. In our absence, the old guards had been relieved, and State troops had taken their place. Before we were turned into the stockade, Lieut. Srofe and myself received our sentence from Col. Brown for attempting to escape. The sentence was, "never to be exchanged, but to remain in prison until the close of the war."

This was a hard blow, and we did not rest until we appealed to the rebel Assistant Agent of Exchange. He gave us poor comfort, and said there was no appeal from the decision that had been made, consequently the sentence would be carried out. He even went farther, and ridiculed us for being re-captured. I met this same Captain after the war in New Orleans, and he had the impudence to tell me that I had not been treated right! I answered him that he might have done a great deal for me at one time, but he failed to do so, therefore I did not want to hear any apologies on the subject.

After we were turned into the stockade we were greeted on all sides by our friends, saying they were very sorry to see us, and the reader can rest assured the feeling was fully reciprocated. In the evening, while surrounded by our old comrades, and relating to them the adventures and misfortunes of our trip, Lieut. Cone, with his glee club, surprised us with a serenade, in honor of our return. The singing had a cheering effect on our drooping spirits, but when they closed the entertainment with the following song, the audience and singers could scarcely suppress a smile:

"Home again! Home again! from a foreign shore,
And oh, it fills my soul with joy,
To meet my friends once more!"

That night, weary and completely worn out, after an absence of one month and twenty-two days, we slept once more in our old bunks. During that time, we had traveled five hundred and seventy-five miles, lived on parched corn a good portion of the time, and last, but not least, we had *missed being exchanged!*

As winter was approaching, farther attempts to escape were impracticable, until the following summer, therefore we tried to make ourselves as comfortable as possible and "bide our time." Our old cabin which we had occupied before we left, was over-crowded with strangers. We therefore did not reclaim our property, but accepted an invitation to live with Mess No. 11, which was composed of the following prisoners : Engineers Bradley and Fales, of the Navy ; Lieut. Harkness, 77th Ill. Infantry ; Joseph Day, of the Chicago Mercantile Battery ; Maj. McCauly, 1st Indiana Cavalry ; Lieut. Srofe and myself. Our shanty was a very poor affair, but before winter set in we built us a new log cabin.

The prison-commander had given the control of all privileges granted to the prisoners, to Capt. J. M. McCullock, 77th Ill. Vols. He was well suited for the position, and did justice to all the prisoners, without fear or favor. Through his influence, we secured the use of a yoke of oxen, to haul logs for our new house. When we had all our timber ready, we tore down the old shanty, and raised our new log cabin, and moved into it the same day. It was ten by twelve feet, and had no windows, depending altogether upon the door for light. We had a clay fire-place, but wood was scarce, and we had to carry nearly all of it over a half-mile, and only had that opportunity a few hours every two weeks.

The weather was very pleasant during the winter, excepting when the Northers raged. They generally came up very suddenly, without any warning, and changed the temperature from a sultry heat to a wintry blast. The wind penetrated through our scant clothing and sent us shiving to our shanties, where we crawled into our bunks and waited until the Norther subsided. They generally lasted from twenty-four to forty-eight hours.

Prison-life had not changed much during our absence. We received our pint of corn-meal and a small piece of beef, daily, excepting on rainy days, when we had to wait for fair weather. Occasionally the arrival of a mail broke the monotony of prison, but it was very seldom that we received any communication from the outside world. I have known cases where prisoners received no word from their families after they were captured, and none of their own letters ever reached home, during their entire imprisonment. On returning home after their release, they learned that they had been mourned as dead, and their families broken up and scattered.

The rebel papers generally gave very glowing accounts of military matters from their stand-point, and converted every defeat into a victory for their arms; therefore the prison authorities sent us their papers regularly, for our perusal, but as we knew what allowance to make for their statements, we were very seldom misled in regard to the true state of affairs.

When I was first captured, I bought two yards of ingrain carpet, for eight dollars, to use in place of a blanket, but when the Regiment was exchanged it was disposed of, which left me without any bedding whatever. In the first days of my captivity I had sold my buck gauntlets to a rebel officer for thirty dollars, and did not know the value of Confederate money until I expended it for ginger-cakes, at one dollar each! The brass buttons on my coat went one at a time, at one dollar each. My watch I had long ago parted with, for forty pounds of bacon. The money received when we passed our Regiment was soon spent, and I was once more penniless, but fortunately I met with an opportunity to borrow one hundred dollars in greenbacks at fifty per cent. interest, payable as soon as I was exchanged. While the money lasted, our mess purchased as much provisions daily as the rebels supplied us with, but after the money was spent we had to fall back on our regular allowance again.

When the day of the Presidential election arrived, Nov. 8th, 1864, the rebel authorities, to ascertain the sentiment of the prisoners, offered us the necessary paper to hold an election in prison. The offer was accepted, and the election was held in due form. I was selected as one of the judges, and still have the original list, with the number of votes of each of the thirteen wards into which the prison was divided. Lincoln received 1,504 votes, and McClellan 687.

Soon after the election, quite a number of roughs, under the leadership of some desperate characters from New York City, armed themselves with clubs, for the purpose of plundering the camp. In open daylight, they drove the peaceful portion of the prisoners out of their quarters, and robbed them of everything found in their cabins. For three or four days they had full sway, but very quietly the "Regulators" prepared their heavy clubs, and the two factions met one afternoon on the principal street. It was a sight long to be remembered, when the two opposing parties, brandishing their clubs, rushed at each other with a yell, and the noise and confusion that arose, as the huge mass swayed back and forth during the melee, was fearful. The roughs were finally overpowered and driven to their quarters, and did not cause any more trouble afterwards. The wounded on both sides were numerous, but none were fatally injured.

Every feasible plan was tried to pass away the time, which hung heavily on our hands. The unvarying sameness of our existence, day after day, bore down upon the mind like a heavy weight, but the suffering incident to the extremes of heat and cold and insufficient food, could be borne better than the mental strain, caused by the close confinement and the ever-recurring thoughts of freedom and home. Our only relief at such times, from an overcharged mind, was to "tramp in the ring," as it was called. The track was in the upper part of the prison, and was 100 yards in circumference. The steady tramp of the prisoners was heard from early morn until late at night. They marched singly and in squads around the circle, until completely worn out, when others took their places, and the endless tramp was continued. As winter approached, the cold weather and scarcity of fuel helped materially to swell the throng.

CHAPTER V.

The Rebel Army Ordered to Richmond, Va.—The Troops Refuse to Cross the Mississippi—Invasion of Missouri —Rebel Soldiers Plundering their Own People—Burial of the Beef—Plot to Overpower the Guards—1,200 Prisoners Exchanged—Their Condition When They Reached New Orleans—The Last Ditch—Foreign Intervention—Lee's Surrender—The War to Last Forty Years Longer—"The Gates Ajar"—The Homeward Journey—Under the Old Flag—Mustered-Out—Description of Camp Ford, Three Months After our Departure—Destruction of Camp Ford.

GEN. KIRBY SMITH, who commanded the rebel forces west of the Mississippi river, received orders from Richmond, Va., during the summer of 1864, to cross the Mississippi river with his whole army, which, according to their own estimates, numbered 60,000 effective men, and march to the relief of Gen. Lee. Some of the troops were started in the direction of the points selected for the crossing, but the soldiers refused to cross under the fire of the gun-boats. The scheme was finally abandoned, and instead, extensive peparations were made to invade Missouri. In the latter part of August, all the arrangements were completed, and the expedition, consisting of three divisions of cavalry, under Maj. Gen. Price, started on the Missouri campaign, that ended so disastrously to the rebel army.

T. C. Reynolds, the rebel Governor of Missouri, accompanied the expedition, for the purpose of re-establishing his authority, if they were successful in holding the State, but they failed, and returned, defeated and badly demoralized, in November. After their return, Governor Reynolds published a letter in the Marshall (Tex.) Republican, of Dec. 23d, 1864, in which he reviewed the causes that led to the failure of the expedition. The principal cause he stated was the lack of discipline, for which he held Gen. Price individually responsible. As the rebels always stigmatized the Union soldiers as robbers and murderers, and exalted the Confederate soldiers as the "Southern Chivalry," therefore the following extract from Governor Reynolds' letter, may be of interest by way of contrast :

"MARSHALL, TEXAS, Dec. 17, 1864.

* * * " It would take a volume to describe the acts of outrage ; neither station, age or sex, was any protection. Southern men and women were as little spared as Unionists. The elegant mansion of Gen. R. E. Lee's accomplished niece, and the cabins of the negro, were alike ransacked. John Deane, the first civilian ever made a State prisoner by Mr. Lincoln's Government, had his watch and money robbed from his person in the streets of Potosi, in broad day, as unceremoniously as the German merchant at Frederickton was forced, a pistol at his ear, to surrender his concealed greenbacks. As the citizens of Arkansas and Northern Texas have seen, in the goods unblushingly offered them for sale, the clothes of the poor man's infant were as attractive spoil as the merchant's silks and calico, or the curtains taken from the rich man's parlor. Ribbons and trumpery gewgaws were stolen from the milliners, and jeweled rings forced from the fingers of delicate maidens, whose brothers were fighting in Georgia in Cockerell's Confederate Missouri brigade.

* * * "The disorders still continued. They may be judged of by the fact, that at Booneville, the hotel occupied as Gen. Price's headquarters was the scene of drunken revelry by night; that guerrillas rode unchecked, in open day, before it, with *human scalps* hanging to their bridles, and tauntingly shaking bundles of plundered greenbacks at our needy soldiers ; and that in an official letter to him there, which he left unanswered and undenied, I asserted, that while 'the wholesale pillage in the vicinity of the army had made it impossible to obtain anything by purchase, stragglers and camp-followers were enriching themselves by plundering the defenseless families of our own soldiers in Confederate service.

"On still darker deeds, I shudderingly keep silent. * * * God-fearing men trembled lest, in Heaven's anger at the excesses which had marked the campaign, some thunderbolt of calamity should fall upon our arms. *It did fall, and like a thunderbolt.* * * *

"THOS. C. REYNOLDS,
"Governor of Missouri."

The Christmas and New Year's holidays came and went, but nothing occurred to break the monotony of our existence, excepting that, in addition to our regular fare, our mess feasted on sweet potatoes and black-eyed peas, which we had purchased from a friendly guard, at the rate of twenty dollars per bushel!

During the winter, our beef was blue and very lean. We notified the prison commander, Col. Perkins, who had relieved Col. Brown, that our beef was not fit to eat, but our complaints were not heeded. The rebels who guarded us, mutinied against receiving such meat, and took one day's rations, consisting of nearly a whole beef, dug a grave, and buried it with the honors of war, not forgetting to fire the parting volley over the grave. From that time their rations were changed to bacon. We could not think of committing such an extravagance as to bury even a single day's rations of tough beef, though we knew that they would be changed afterward for the better.

In the latter part of January, 1865, I received a notice to attend a secret meeting, in the cabin occupied by the officers of the 130th Ills. At dark, I went to the place where the meeting was to be held. I found the door strongly guarded, and sentinels posted outside, to give the alarm in case of any outside intrusion. After some delay I was admitted, and as I entered, a Kansas Captain was making an eloquent appeal to a crowded house, urging the prisoners to overpower the guards, mount themselves with the horses belonging to the guards, and others that could be found in the vicinity, and strike for the land of freedom. Quite a number of other speakers followed, who were the leaders in the plot, and any one who attempted to say a word against the proposition was hissed down and denounced as a coward. My opinion was that it was a very dangerous project. I had seen a portion of the rebel army after my re-capture, that would confront us, even if we succeeded in overpowering the prison-guards. But I dare not express my real opinion before such an audience.

At length I was called upon to express my views upon the subject. I remarked that they could depend on me in anything they would undertake, to get out of prison, but I would not go into anything blindly. I considered it a very serious business. I wanted them to investigate the matter in regard to the number of horses that we could get in the neighborhood, and how many arms were stored in Tyler, etc.; then we might talk of action, and not before. My remarks had the desired effect, and it was immediately moved that a committee of three be appointed to get all the necessary information, to enable us to make our escape *"en masse."* I was placed on the committee, and by making a show of great energy I had it all my own way. I kept putting off my report from day to day under various pretexts, in order to gain time, until finally I hardly knew what excuse to offer for any further delay, when orders were received to forward 1,200 prisoners for exchange, and the prospect was that more would soon follow, which nipped the plot in the bud.

Our Government sent us a lot of clothing, which was received on the first of February, and was distributed only to the most needy. From the boxes that the clothing was packed in, several new industries sprang up. From the strap-iron around the boxes, table-knives were manufactured, and from the lumber, violins were made.

To Lieut. Paine, of the 18th New York Cavalry, I am indebted for a fine violin. He plied his trade for two months to good advantage, on the instrument, his only tool being the broken blade of a knife. He presented the violin to me when he and Capt. Dill made their escape. They started for the coast, and got within sight of the gunboats, when they were re-captured and taken to Houston, Texas, and held until the close of the war.

Feb. 10th, 1200 prisoners were exchanged. The following is an extract from the Cincinnati Commercial, of March 11th, 1865, written by their New Orleans correspondent, which gives a faithful description of the condition of the prisoners when they reached our lines:

"NEW ORLEANS, Feb. 28, 1865.

"The first prisoners of the new regulation for exchange, were received here day before yesterday, the 77th Ohio, 36th Iowa, and portions of other regiments, arriving here from Texas.

"From Capt. McCormick, 77th Ohio, and the Prison Hospital Steward, T. J. Robinson, of the 36th Iowa, I have learned a few facts, regarding the situation and treatment while in prison at Tyler, Texas. It is an oft-told tale—the same sad narrative of abuse and privation which has become in this war, alas! so common.

"Most of the men were taken at Marks' Mills, Ark., and as soon as they had been marched to the rear, they were systematically and completely stripped of everything—hats, blankets, boots, etc. Arrived at Tyler, 4,300 were crowded into a stockade of four acres, on a hill-side, without anything to protect them from the dews, rain or sun. Without a blanket, or a shingle, or even a dry bough of a tree, to screen themselves, they were told, in mockery, to "make themselves as comfortable as possible."

With an old ax, a saw and an auger, they built two wretched pens, covered partly with brush and partly with puncheons, for the accommodation of the sick. They had not a nail or a board, or any straw, with which to make bunks for them. In these miserable abodes, there were generally from 120 to 160 sick at a time. To these there was issued enough quinine and the commonest drugs, for about twenty men, and the rebel surgeon, appointed to have them in charge during the last six weeks, came to look after them twice.

"There was an absolute lack of every comfort. 'Many a poor fellow,' said the Steward to me, 'has died in the night, when we had not even the light of a tallow candle to close his eyes.' The rations, to all alike, sick and well, were corn-meal and beef. In the summer the beef was good, but after the frost had cut down the prairie-grass, it rapidly grew blue and lean. These men have arrived here just in the condition in which they left Camp Ford, and are now quartered at the camp of distribution. Three or four of them died on the way down, so worn and wasted were they, after months of suffering in that place of torments.

"It stirs one's blood like a trumpet, to grasp these honest veterans of many a battle by the hand, hard and bony though it be—these bronzed and battered lads—and hear their manly voices. But move on a little farther, and look on the other hand at the sad, wan faces of these others, who sit silent and gaze about them, or upon their new-found friends, with a look of vacant wonder—almost idiocy—demented, and brought to the edge of the grave by their captors. Is it strange or foolish, if strong men speak with a quivering voice, and turn away, that they may hide a tear, when they look upon these poor wretches? Let him not be thought weak or unmanly who is thus moved, for he must be indeed something more or less than human who could do otherwise. * *

" Maj. Bering and Lieut. Srofe, of the 48th Ohio, were detained by the rebel exchange officer at Camp Ford, he claiming that they had forfeited their right to be exchanged, in consequence of having attempted to escape. It will occur to most persons, that this is a singular pretext to advance for such a proceeding. Q. P. F."

As spring advanced, our hope of release was based mainly on the prospect that the war would soon come to a close, which began to look like a possibility after Hood's defeat at Nashville, Price's defeat in Missouri, and "Sherman's March to the Sea." Their boast, to "die in the last ditch," rather than come back into the Union, was heard no more ; but instead, they were eagerly looking for some foreign power to take up their cause, and deliver them from Yankee subjugation.

The rebel Gen. R. Taylor says : " There was much talk about setting up a government west of the Mississippi, uniting with Maximilian, and calling on Louis Napoleon for assistance."

Another Southern historian states :

" H. W. Allen, Governor of Louisiana, had dispatched Gen. Polignac with communications to Napoleon III., Emperor of the French, and it was desirable, above all things, to keep the Confederate flag afloat yet a few months longer. It has since been ascertained, that two or three months more of resistance would have brought recognition, and the salvation of the Confederacy."

They were prepared to bow the knee to the sceptre of any foreign monarch, who would have helped them out of the dilemma into which their short-sighted leaders had led them. Such was the sentiment of their citizens and soldiers, with whom we came in contact at that stage of the war. Yet at times, they were defiant as ever, and almost persuaded us that the war had but fairly commenced. The gloomy outlook of their cause had its effect on the prison authorities, which caused them to relax their severity, and occasionally they would grant us some favors.

North of the prison, was a field of about ten acres, but as the rebels had burned all the rails, the field was of no benefit to them. Capt. John Watts, of the 130th Ills. Vols., an old, grey-haired veteran, proposed to Col. Perkins, the prison commander, that if he would let him out every day, with twenty-five men, he would go the woods, make rails, carry them to the field, fence up a portion, and plant it in corn and beans, for the benefit of those who agreed to do the work. Col. Perkins gave his consent, with the proviso that every man give his word of honor not to attempt to escape while at work.

On the first spring day, "Uncle John," as the Captain was generally called, took out his men and went to work. In a short time he had sufficient ground fenced in to raise a crop. He then procured a plow, attached twenty men to it, and broke up the ground. But Gen. Grant spoiled the

Captain's calculations about raising a crop in Texas, when he forced Gen. Lee and his army to surrender. " Uncle John" had to come away and leave his farm in a flourishing condition, and I suppose he has never forgiven Gen. Grant for not giving him time to reap the fruits of his industry.

In the latter part of April, the rebel papers contained the news that President Lincoln had been assassinated. We considered it a joke, at the time, for the reason that they had published a similar report about six months previous; but gradually it came in such a shape that we could no longer doubt it. It cast a gloom over the prison that cannot easily be forgotten. Their papers were silent for some time in regard to Lee's surrender, which had taken place before the assassination.

At last it was whispered around among the guards that Gen. Grant had really captured Gen. Lee's whole army. At this news our joy knew no bounds, but in a few days afterward, their papers, in speaking of the disaster that had befallen their arms in Virginia, stated that it did not affect the territory west of the Mississippi River, and that they could "hold out for forty years longer!" The papers also contained the proclamation of General Kirby Smith, in which he stated that all they had to do was to hold out faithfully, and they would yet gain their independence. That was rather a damper on our buoyant spirits ; but fortunately, our rebel guards could not see it in that light, but packed their baggage, and in the night of May 14th, like the Arabs of old, they "folded their tents and silently stole away." Our feelings can better be imagined than described, when on the following morning we found the "Gates Ajar"—not a solitary sentinel on guard, and the rebel camp deserted! But strange to stay, not a cheer was given, nor did a single yell awake the echoes of the surrounding hills. The prisoners went about with a dazed, stupefied stare. They were actually afraid to trust their own senses, for fear it would turn out to be only a delusion.

It was some time before any one ventured outside the stockade, and when we did find out that we were free to go where we pleased, comrades met comrades with a firm grasp of the hand, eyes moist with tears, and hearts too full for utterance, except a fervent "Thank God!"

But the great war of the rebellion was drawing to a close. Maj. Gen. Pope had already demanded the surrender of the Trans-Mississippi Department. Then followed the negotiations, but before a formal surrender could be agreed upon, the Texas troops held a conference, and resolved to disband and go home, and began to make preparations to carry out their plans. The cavalry disbanded next, and plundered the country on their route. The Government warehouses and manufactories were destroyed and set on fire. The extensive Government works at Tyler were threatened by a mob, but the rebel soldiers appropriated the bulk of the supplies for their own use.

On May 16th, some rebel officers made arrangements to send us to New Orleans, but before we left, a number of the prisoners volunteered to enclose the cemetery with a fence, where over 300 of our men lay buried, thus paying them the last tribute of respect that lay in our power. Among the foremost in this undertaking, was Lieutenant H. Wyman, of the 77th Illinois.

May 17th, all the prisoners, numbering about 1200 men, composed of the 120th Ohio, 77th and 130th Ills. regiments, and small squads from various commands, started for Shreveport, accompanied by a battalion of rebel cavalry, who volunteered to escort us to our lines, provided that we would intercede and get favorable terms of surrender for them. When we reached our lines, we found that our services were not required, as the conditions of the surrender of all Confederate soldiers were more liberal than they would have asked, if left to them to make their own terms.

We made very slow progress on our journey, for the reason that the country was full of disbanded rebel soldiers, returning to their homes. We had secured a number of teams, to haul our provisions and sick; but the rebel soldiers confiscated our mules and left us standing in the road, with our wagons. They said they had not been paid off for two years, and they were determined to have something. As often as we procured new teams, they were taken from us. Finally, after considerable delay, we reached Shreveport, and camped in the suburbs. The rebel soldiers had attempted to burn the city the night previous to our arrival, in which they had partly succeeded.

The following day, several of the Missouri officers, who had treated us so kindly at Washington, Ark., paid us a visit. They seemed to be very much depressed at the state of affairs, but more particularly as they expected harsh treatment, should they fall into the hands of the Federal authorities, and no doubt that was the principal cause of so many leaving for Mexico, before the surrender took place.

In a few days, we embarked on the steamboats and landed at the mouth of Red River, May 27th, where we were transferred to our steamers, under the "old flag," once more. We had become accustomed to the slim diet of the Confederacy during our fourteen months imprisonment, and were well aware of the danger if we lost control of our appetites when we reached our lines, therefore quite a number resolved to eat very sparingly for the first eight or ten days; but when the gong sounded for dinner, after we had been transferred to our boats, the prisoners, without exception, could be restrained no longer, but rushed into the cabin, casting all their resolutions to the winds, and ate to their hearts' content.

The following day, we reached New Orleans, where the rebel Generals, Buckner and Price, who had accompanied us from Shreveport, surrendered to Gen. Canby, the Trans-Mississippi Department, which completed the transfer of all the so-called Confederate States, to the United States authorities.

The rest is soon told. The war being over, all the prisoners, with but few exceptions, were mustered out of the service and sent home. Among the latter, I was included, which terminated my military career.

The following letter from the New York Tribune gives a graphic description of " Camp Ford," three months after our departure.

THE REBEL PRISON AT CAMP FORD—A SECOND ANDERSONVILLE.

NEW YORK, Aug. 18, 1865.—The Tribune's Tyler (Texas) correspondent describes Camp Ford, near that place, a prison-pen, second only to Andersonvile in the barbarism and atrocities inflicted upon Union prisoners for two years. The correspondent says :

" Scourged, beaten and tortured, these prisoners were too far off, and too closely guarded, for their groans to be heard by those in the outside world. Their sad story only became known from their own shrunken lips, after they had been exchanged. It is a stockaded enclosure of about, I judge, eight or ten acres. This estimate includes all adjuncts of the prison. It is situated on the side of a sandy slope, at the lower edge of which, and just within the stockade, is a spring that supplied water to the prisoners. The enclosure, which seems to have been enlarged at different times, to meet the requirements of rebel captures, is filled with huts and shanties of almost every imaginable shape, and constructed of every available material.

"Two barrels, one on top of the other, form the chimney of a hut made of bushes, the limbs of which have been pressed together and plastered with mud. Near the point at which we entered, there is a number of grave-like mounds, scattered over the space of about one acre. I at first thought they were graves, but on examining, I found they were excavations in the ground, which had been covered, first with bushes, and then with dirt. They had been made by those of our men who had been captured last, and for whom there was no room in the huts above ground. Everywhere are blackened spots, which show where their fires had formerly been, by means of which those who had no shelter at all, cooked their daily mite of meat. Fragments of kettles and stoves, old cast-off pans, and flat rocks, the cooking utensils they had used, were strewn about, and, as I noticed in one of the huts, piled up with care to await future use.

"Toward the upper side of the enclosure, where there seems to have been a prison for the confinement of officers, are several stumps, on the top of which those who violated any of the prison rules were made to stand and mark time, for perhaps a whole day, while the guard had imperative orders to shoot any one who stopped, or fell off from exhaustion. The whole scene, with its associations, is a horrid illustration of the inhumanity that originated and carried on the rebellion until its overthrow. Perhaps I am raking a hurtful coal from dead ashes, so I will stop."

EXIT "CAMP FORD."

While writing the closing events at Camp Ford, a letter lies before me, from Lieut. W. J. Srofe, written at Galveston, Texas, Dec. 21st, 1865, in which he says :

* * "I saw Maj. Thos. D. Vredenburg,* of the 10th Ill. Cavalry, a short time ago. He had just arrived from Shreveport with his command, 'via Camp Ford.' He made a halt at the stockade, and his bump of destructiveness was so great as to prompt him to leave it in ruins. Ah, my good fellow, it almost makes me shed tears to think of that master-piece of architecture, our old home, being thus ruthlessly destroyed by 'vandal hands.' When I think of the 'happy hours' spent beneath its roof, the 'delicious feasts' served up within its walls, and 'refreshing' slumbers upon its 'downy' beds, where we dreamed of pleasures, and the dear ones at home, it is too much to bear, and I think he deserves the censure of all the old residents of Camp Ford!" * * *

---
* An old Camp Ford Prisoner.

APPENDIX.

Additional List of Killed and Wounded of the 48th Ohio Vet. Vols.—List of Officers of the 13th Army Corps, Prisoners at Camp Ford, Texas—Roster of the Commissioned Officers of the 48th Ohio Vet. Vols.

PARTIAL LIST of Killed and wounded of the 48th Regiment at the battle of Shiloh, April 6th and 7th, 1862, as far as we could ascertain:

COMPANY A.

Killed: Clem Tudor, David Morgan, Elias Henry.

Wounded: Sergeants William Willis and B. W. Ladd. Corporals Geo. R. Conard and Daniel T. Williams. Privates W. C. Edwards, John W. Spurlock, David Woosley, J. W. Leeka, Peter Fry.

Missing: Chas. Rodgers.

Taken Prisoner: Wm. Tudor.

COMPANY B.

Killed: Aaron Sales.

Mortally Wounded: Elias J. Hill, Wm. James and L. Malott.

Wounded Severely: First Serg't. John D. Nevins, Corp'l. W. N. Harvey and Simeon Sales.

Slightly Wounded: James Brewer.

COMPANY C.

Killed: Jesse Nelson.

Mortally Wounded: Jacob Lippolt, Simpson Rains and John C. Hamontree.

Severely Wounded: James Vanpelt, Edward Chambers, Amos Laymon, L. A. Williams, E. Jones, James Seal and D. B. Hogan.

Slightly Wounded: W. A. Pratt, J. W. Hayner.

Taken Prisoners: J. W. Hayner, E. Lafferty.

COMPANY D.

Killed: Serg't. John Canter, Peter Craven, Bushrod McDonald and Milton Pavey.

Mortally Wounded and Taken Prisoner: Albert West.

Slightly Wounded: David H. Canter and Corp'l. John T. McElvain.

COMPANY E.

Killed: Isaac Duncan and I. Fox.

Wounded: Henry Lair, Obed Macy, — Lendersmith and Henry Hilderbrand.

COMPANY F.

Wounded: Edwin Cory, Christopher Nagle, George Morrison, Robert Cosgrave, James Myers, Frederick Hoeltzel and David Welker.

COMPANY G.

Killed: Richard Smith.

Slightly Wounded: James Hair.

COMPANY H.

Mortally Wounded: Corporals Stephen Workman and John Bardsley.

APPENDIX. 275

COMPANY I.

Killed: Privates, S. Hallam, Jacob Thomas, Selkirk Molott, Wilson Kratzer and E. Hill.

Mortally Wounded: First Serg't. P. M. Everhard.

Wounded: Corporal Moses Edwards. Privates Geo. Weeks and Cornelius Turner.

COMPANY K.

Killed: Samuel Doty and Hiram S. Manchester.

Mortaily Wounded: Wm. J. Helmes, John Riley.

Wounded: Serg't. W. J. Srofe, Corp'l. B. C. Bourne, F. L. Ashton, Jno. Hitesman, Wm. B. Kennedy and John McKenzie.

Partial list of killed and wounded at Arkansas Post, Jan. 11, 1863:

COMPANY B.

Wounded: James Brewer, J. J. Thompson.

COMPANY D.

Wounded: Corporals Allen Pierce, John T. McElvain and H. Luttrell.

COMPANY E.

Wounded: D. Craven.

COMPANY F.

Killed: George Blair.

COMPANY H.

Wounded: Serg't. Geo. M. Williams and Corp'l. Michael Stark.

COMPANY K.

Killed : John W. Daily.
Wounded : James H. Troy.

Killed and wounded at Ft. Blakely, Alabama, April 9, 1865, giving the letter of the company to which they belonged in the 48th Ohio before the consolidation :

COMPANY B.

Mortally Wounded : John R. Lynn.

COMPANY C.

Wounded : Corp'l. Allen Turnipseed.

COMPANY D.

Killed : H. Cox.
Wounded : J. W. Cashatt and Geo. Cox.

COMPANY G.

Wounded : Corp'l. W. C. Robins.

COMPANY H.

Wounded : Riley Workman, received nine wounds and recovered.

COMPANY K.

Wounded : Elias Conover, William Lindsey.

LIST OF OFFICERS 13TH ARMY CORPS, AT CAMP FORD PRISON, TEXAS.

The following is a list of the officers of the 13th Army Corps, captured at Sabine Cross-Roads, La., April 8, 1864. Also those of the 77th Ohio, captured at Marks' Mills, and 120th Ohio, captured on steamer City Belle :

19TH KENTUCKY VOL. INF.

Lieut. Col. John Cowan, Danville, Kentucky.
Maj. J. I. Mann, Harrodsburg, "
Adj't. Geo. C. Rue, " "
Capt. Wm. H. Cundiff, Somerset, "
" L. A. Hamblin, "
" Henry L. Whitehouse, Haysville,"
" John Barnett, Antioch, "
" H. H. Forbes, Danville, "
" Alexander Logan, Lancaster, "
" W. F. McKinney, Stanford, "
Lieut. V. L. Lester, Somerset, "
" Thomas Cundiff, " "
" Abe Whitnack, Harrodsburg, "
" Elijah Baker, Poor Fork, "
" Eberle Wilson, Hustonville, "
" Zachariah Morgan, Hazard, "
" S. W. Hedger, Lancaster, "

130TH ILLINOIS VOL. INF.

Capt. Wm. Prescott, Springfield, Illinois.
" Jesse R. Johnson, Claremont, "
" John W. Watts, Sumner, "
. Lieut. J. W. Paulin, Curran, "

Lieut. Wm. Harnerd, Pocahontas, Illinois.
" R. S. Taylor, Springfield, "
" Wm. C. Pool, Marshall, "
" Chas. W. Johnson, Pocahontas, "

77TH ILLINOIS VOL. INF.

Capt. J. M. McCullock, Low Point, Illinois.
" Joseph H. Stevison, Peoria, "
" G. G. Stearns, Knoxville, "
Lieut. H. L. Bushnell, Peoria, "
" M. O. Harkness, Southport, "
" S. S. Edwards, Edwards Station, "
" Henry Wyman, Brimfield, "
" C. F. McCullock, Low Point, "
Chaplain J. S. McCullock, Peoria, "

48TH OHIO VET. VOL. INF.

Lieut. Col. J. W. Lindsey, Delaware, Ohio.
Maj. J. A. Bering, Lynchburg, "
Capt. James Sowry, West Milton, "
" Daniel Gunsaullus, Fayette, Kansas.
" Andrew M. Cochran, Greenville, O.
" Thos. Montgomery, Lynchburg, "
Lieut. M. McCaffrey, New Lexington, "
" Wm. J. Srofe, Hamersville, "
" Harvey W. Day, Mt. Oreb, "

MISCELLANEOUS COMMANDS.

Lieut. P. S. Evans, 96th Ohio, Marysville, O.
" Nicholas Steinauer, 60th Ind. Tell City, Indiana.
" S. W. Griffith, 32d Iowa, Berlin, Iowa.
Capt. P. H. White, Chic. Mer. Bat., Albany, N. Y.

APPENDIX. 279

Lieut. P. S. Cone, same, Chicago, Ill.
Lieut. Col. A. M. Flora, 46th Ind., Logansport, Indiana.
Capt. Wm. DeHart, same, Logansport, Ind.
Chap. Hamilton Robb, same, Delphi, Ind.
Lieut. Thos. Hughes, 28th Ia., Iowa City, Ia.

120TH OHIO VOL. INF.

Captured on steamer City Belle, at Snaggy Point, Louisiana, May 3, 1864:

Capt. J. P. Rummell, Newville, Ohio.
" Benj. G. Miller, Wooster, "
" Elias Froundfelter, Ashland, "
" Benj. G. Jones, Shreve, "
Capt. Valentine Moffat, Dalton, "
Lieut. Harvey Applegate, Perryville, "
" Wm. B. Millikan, Ontario, "

77TH OHIO VOL. INF.

Captured at Marks' Mills, April 25, 1864:
Capt. A. W. McCormack, Cincinnati, Ohio.
" R. H. McKitrich, " "
Lieut. R. E. Smithson, Regnier's Mills, "
" Sam'l. Fulton, Clarington, "
" R. H. Flemming, Barlow, "
" Wm. W. Scott, Barlow, "
" N. B. Smith, McConnellsville, "
" D. A. Marlow, Matamoras, "

ROSTER OF COMMISSIONED OFFICERS OF THE FORTY-EIGHTH O. V. V. I.

Rank.	Name.	Commission Issued.	Remarks.
Colonel	Peter J. Sullivan	Feb. 29, 1862.	Resigned Aug. 7th, 1863. Breveted Brigadier General March 13th, 1865.
"	Job R. Parker	Mar. 18, 1864.	Mustered out Jan. 17th, 1865. Died Dec. 5th, 1865.
Lieut. Col.	Peter J. Sullivan	Feb. 29, 1862.	Promoted to Colonel.
"	Job R. Parker	" 28, "	"
"	Joseph W. Lindsey	Aug. 20, 1863.	Mustered out Jan. 17th, 1865.
"	James R. Lynch	Sept. 4, 1865.	Mustered out with the Regiment May 9, 1866.
Major	James S. Wise	Feb. 21, 1862.	Resigned Sept. 3d, 1862.
"	S. G. W. Peterson	" 6, 1863	Revoked; resigned as Captain Feb. 21st, 1863.
"	Virgil H. Monts	Mar. 25, 1863.	Mortally wounded May 22d, 1863. Died July 11, 1863.
"	John A. Bering	Jan. 27, 1864.	Mustered out June 16, 1865.
Surgeon	Milton F. Cary	Feb. 28, 1862.	Resigned March 11, 1863.
"	Plyn A. Willis	Mar. 11, 1863.	Was appointed Medical Director on the staff of Gen. Andrews in the spring of 1865. Resigned March 10, 1866. Died April 18, 1876.
Ass't Surg.	A. A. Johnson	Feb. 25, 1862.	Resigned March 8, 1863.
"	John K. Lewis	Aug. 25, 1862.	Died Oct. 11, 1862.
"	Plyn A. Willis	Dec. 2, 1862.	Promoted to Surgeon.
"	C. Homer Wiles	April 4, 1863.	Mustered out July 25, 1865.
"	William Watt	" 16, 1863.	Resigned Jan. 6, 1864.
Chaplain	John F. Spence	Feb. 28, 1862.	Resigned March 18, 1863.
Captain	Job R. Parker	" 28, "	Promoted to Lieut.-Colonel.
"	J. W. Frazee	" 28, "	Resigned Jan. 14, 1863.
"	John J. Ireland	" 28, "	Died March 16, 1862.
"	Cyrus Elwood	" 28, "	Discharged Nov. 1, 1862.
"	S. G. W. Peterson	" 28, "	Resigned Feb. 21, 1863.
"	W. L. Warner	" 28, "	Killed April 7, 1862.
"	Virgil H. Monts	" 28, "	Promoted to Major.
"	George A. Miller	" 28, "	Resigned June 6, 1862.

APPENDIX.

Rank.	Name.	Commission Issued.	Remarks.
Captain	J. E. Bond	Feb. 28, 1862.	Mortally wounded April 6. Died April 22, 1862.
"	Isaac J. Ross	" 23, "	Resigned Dec. 10, 1862.
"	Richard A. Robins	" 28, "	Resigned Feb. 14, 1863.
"	J. W. Lindsey	June 21, 1862.	Promoted to Lieut.-Colonel.
"	George A. Miller	Sept. 12, 1862.	Resigned June 10, 1863.
"	Francis M. Posegate	Oct. 3, 1862.	" " 25, "
"	James C. Kelsey	Feb. 6, 1863.	" Feb. 20, "
"	John A. Bering	" 4, "	Promoted to Major.
"	Joshua Hussey	" 6, "	Resigned as 1st Lieutenant Feb. 15, 1863.
"	Richard T. Wilson	" 6, "	Resigned April 12, 1863.
"	James Sowrey	Mar. 25, 1863.	Mustered out Jan. 17, 1865.
"	Cyrus Hussey	" 25, "	" "
"	Isaac L. Tice	May 28, 1863.	Resigned Sept., 1863.
"	Robert T. Coverdale	Jan. 25, 1864.	Promoted to Captain A. Q. M. Sept. 19, 1864.
"	Daniel Guneaullus	Mar. 25, 1863.	Resigned Feb., 1865.
"	Cyrus P. Bratt	Jan. 25, 1864.	Resigned Mar. 27, 1864.
"	Andrew M. Cochran	" 25, "	Mustered out with the Regiment May 9, 1866.
"	James R. Lynch	" 25, "	Promoted to Lieut.-Colonel.
"	Thomas Montgomery	" 25, "	Mustered out Jan. 17, 1865.
"	Richard A. South	" 25, "	Revoked. Resigned as 1st Lieutenant.
"	George W. Mosgrove	" 25, "	Mustered out with the Regiment May 9, 1866, and died in Texas in 1867.
"	Michael McCaffrey	May 2, 1865.	Mustered out with the Regiment May 9, 1866. Died since muster-out.
1st Lieut.	Wm. H. H. Rike	Sept. 4, 1865.	Mustered out with Regiment May 9, 1866.
"	Richard A. Robins	Feb. 28, 1862.	Promoted to Captain.
"	S. G. W. Peterson	" 28, "	"
"	J. C. Kelsey	" 28, "	"
"	Joshua Hussey	" 28, "	Promoted. Resigned Feb. 15, 1863.
"	John J. Greer	" 28, "	Resigned March 3, 1863
"	Jos. W. Lindsey	" 28, "	Promoted to Captain.
"	Aquilla Conard	" 28, "	Resigned July 16, 1862.

APPENDIX.

Rank	Name	Date	Notes
1st Lieut.	Chas. A. Partridge	Feb. 28, 1862.	Resigned Jan. 23, 1863.
"	Wm. A. Quarterman	" 28, "	" " 25, "
"	Francis M. Posegate	" 28, "	Promoted to Captain
"	Isaac L. Tice	" 28, "	Discharged Dec. 10, 1862. Restored.
"	Wm. E. Brayman	" 28, "	Resigned Feb. 21, 1863.
"	Robert C. McGill	" 29, 1862.	" Aug. 2, "
"	Richard T. Wilson	Mar. 20, 1862.	Promoted to Captain.
"	David R. Plyly	June 24, 1862.	Resigned Oct. 1863.
"	James Sowrey	Dec. 31, 1862.	Promoted to Captain.
"	Robert T. Coverdale	Dec. 31, 1862.	"
"	Cyrus P. Bratt	Feb. 6, 1863.	"
"	G. W. Mosgrove	" 6, "	"
"	Cyrus Hussey	" 6, "	"
"	Daniel Gnusaullus	Mar. 25, 1863.	Resigned Sept. 16, 1863.
"	Andrew M. Cochran	Feb. 6, "	Resigned Dec. 16, 1861.
"	James R. Lynch	Mar. 25, "	Promoted to Captain.
"	Cornelius Conard	Mar. 25, 1863.	"
"	Peter Brown	" 25, "	"
"	Thomas Montgomery	Mar. 25, 1863.	Mustered out, May 24, 1864.
"	Wm. H. Rike	" 25, "	Resigned Jan. 9, 1864.
"	Michael McCaffrey	" 25, "	Mustered out Jan. 17, 1865.
"	Wm. H. Smith	" 25, "	Revoked. Deceased 2d Lieutenant.
"	Richard A. South	Jan. 25, 1864.	
"	Harvey W. Day	" 25, "	Revoked; resigned 2d Lieutenant.
"	Thos. W. Wright	" 25, "	
"	John K. Reed	" 25, "	Mustered out with Regiment May 9, 1866.
"	John M. Kendall	" 25, "	Killed April 8, 1864.
"	Jesse H. Allison	" 25, "	Resigned July 25, 1865.
"	Wm. J. Srole	" 25, "	"
"	Christian Burkhart	" 25, "	"
"	Jos. Stretch	" 21, "	"
"	George L. Byers	Nov. 21, "	Mustered out with Regiment May 9, 1866.
"	Benj. W. Ladd	" 26, "	"

APPENDIX.

Rank.	Name.	Commission Issued.	Remarks.
1st Lieut.	Frank M. Swaney	Sept. 4, 1865.	Mustered out with Regiment, May 9, 1866.
"	Samuel H. Stevenson	" 4, "	"
"	John Wilson	Nov. 26, 1864.	"
"	John M. Wilson	May 2, 1865.	"
2d Lieut.	F. M. Posegate	Feb. 28, 1862.	Promoted to 1st Lieutenant.
"	John Kean	" 29, "	Discharged Sept. 8, 1862.
"	Robert T. Coverdale	" 28, "	Promoted to 1st Lieutenant.
"	T. L. Fields	" 28, "	Resigned Sept. 6, 1862. Died Sept. 29, 1862.
"	R. T. Wilson	" 28, "	Promoted to 1st Lieutenant.
"	James Sowrey	" 28, "	"
"	G. W. Mosgrove	" 28, "	"
"	Cyrus P. Bratt	" 28, "	"
"	Daniel Gunsaullus	" 28, "	"
"	David R. Plyly	" 28, "	"
"	Cyrus Hussey	" 28, "	"
"	Andrew M. Cochran	Dec. 31, 1862.	"
"	Thomas Montgomery	Feb. 4, 1863.	"
"	W. H. H. Rike	Mar. 6, "	"
"	Michael McCuffrey	Feb. 6, "	"
"	Cornelius Conard	" 6, "	"
"	W. H. Smith	Mar. 6, "	Promoted to 1st Lieutenant.
"	James R. Lynch	Feb. 6, "	"
"	Richard A. South	Mar. 6, "	"
"	Harvey W. Day	" 25, "	"
"	Thos. W. Wright	Feb. 24, "	Died May 10, 1863, at Raymond, Miss.
"	John K. Reed	Mar. 25, "	Promoted to 1st Lieutenant.
"	John M. Kendall	" 25, "	Resigned Feb. 24, 1864.
"	Jesse H. Allison	" 25, "	Resigned Sept. 17, 1863.
"	Wm J. Srofe	" 25, "	Promoted to 1st Lieutenant.
"	James Douglass	Sept. 4, 1865.	Mustered out with the Regiment May 9, 1866.
"	Thomas H. Hansell	" 4, "	"
"	Asa N. Ballard	" 4, "	"

ROSTER OF COMPANY C, FORTY-EIGHTH REGIMENT O. V. V. I.

COMMISSIONED OFFICERS.

Rank	Name	Date of Commission Issued	Remarks
Captain	J. W. Frazee	Oct. 15, 1861	Resigned Jan. 14, 1863.
"	J. A. Bering*†	Jan. 14, 1863	Promoted to Major Jan. 25, 1864. Mustered out June 16, 1865.
"	Thomas Montgomery*†	" 25, 1864.	Mustered out by reason of consolidation Jan. 17, '65.
1st Lieut.	Peter Brown	Oct. 15, 1861.	Resigned Dec 16, 1861.
"	Wm. A. Quarterman	Jan. 1, 1862.	Resigned Jan. 25, 1863.
"	Thomas Montgomery	Feb. 21, 1863.	Promoted to Captain.
2d Lieut.	T. L. Fields	Oct. 15, 1861.	Resigned Sept. 6, 1862. Died Sept. 29, 1862.
"	Thomas Montgomery	Jan. 14, 1863.	Promoted to 1st Lieutenant.

NON-COMMISSIONED OFFICERS.

Rank	Name	When Enlisted	When Promoted	Promoted
1st Serg't	W. A. Quarterman	Oct. 3, 1861.	Oct. 14, 1861.	Promoted to 1st Lieutenant.
"	J. A. Bering	" 3, "	Jan. 1, 1862.	Promoted to Captain.
"	W. A. Pratt	" 3, "	" 14, 1863.	Promoted to Sergeant Major.
"	S. F. Prickett*†	" 3, "	Mar. 1, 1864.	Mustered out as supernumerary, Jan. 17, 1865.
Sergeant	W. A. Pratt	" 3, "	Oct. 14, 1861.	Promoted to 1st Sergeant.
"	J. A. Bering	" 3, "	" 14, "	"
"	Emanuel Kelso	" 3, "	" 14, "	Transferred to Co. H, Jan. 1st, 1862.
"	J. F. Holladay	" 3, "	" 14, "	Wounded March 12, 1863. Discharged July 23d, 1863.
"	S. F. Prickett†	" 3, "	Jan. 1, 1862.	Promoted to 1st Sergeant.
"	Thomas Montgomery	" 3, "	" 1, "	Promoted to 2d Lieutenant.
"	Wm. M. Blshir†	" 16, "	May 1, "	Mustered out by reason of expiration of term.

		When Enlisted.	When Promoted.	
Sergeant	Chas. Weber	Oct. 3, 1861.	Apr. 12, 1863.	Killed at Vicksburg, May 22d, 1863.
"	J. D. Leonard	" 3, "	" 12, "	Mustered out by reason of expiration of term.
"	Hugh Dunseith* †	" 3, "	May 28, "	Mustered out as supernumerary, Jan. 17, 1865.
"	Harvey Cashatt*	Dec 7, "	Mar. 1, 1864.	Mustered out April 4, 1866, at Columbus, O.
"	George S. Smith* †	Oct. 3, "	Jan. 1, 1865.	Mustered out with Regiment May 10, 1866.
Corporal	George Bishir* †	" 3, "	" 1, "	Promoted to Sergeant.
"	S. F. Prickett	" 3, "	Oct. 14, 1861.	Mustered out as supernumerary Jan. 17, 1865.
"	Japhet Wayne* †	" 3, "	" 14, "	Promoted to Sergeant.
"	George Bishir	" 3, "	" 14, "	" "
"	George S. Smith	" 3, "	" 14, "	" "
"	Samuel L. L. Spees	" 3, "	" 14, "	Discharged for disability May 1, 1862.
"	Thomas Montgomery	Oct. 3, "	" 14, "	Promoted to Sergeant.
"	W. C. Wondrow	" 3, "	" 14, "	Discharged for disability Nov. 22, 1861.
"	J. D. Leonard	" 3, "	" 14, "	Promoted to Sergeant.
"	W. M. Bishir	" 16, "	Nov. 23, "	" "
"	Charles Weber	" 3, "	Jan. 1, 1862.	Discharged for disability Nov. 11, 1862.
"	A. J. Swaim	" 3, "	" 1, "	Mortally wounded, April 8, 1864.
"	Samuel Hair*	" 14, "	" 1, "	Promoted to Sergeant.
"	Hugh Dunseith	" 3, "	May 1, "	" "

PRIVATES.

	When Enlisted.	
Aber John	Oct. 3, 1861.	Discharged Nov. 11, 1862.
Aber William	" 4, "	Died of typhoid fever, April 23, 1862, at Cincinnati, O.
Barnett R. B.* †	" 3, "	Mustered out with the Regiment.
Beard Charles	" 3, "	Transferred to invalid corps Oct. 29, 1863.
Boyland Patrick	" 7, "	Discharged Feb. 22, 1864.
Barker Samuel* †	" 8, "	Mustered out with the Regiment.
Barker Elias* †	" 8, "	" " "
Barker A. J.	" 14, "	" expiration of term.
Bardsley J. W.	Dec. 27, "	{Transferred to Co. H, Jan. 1, 1862. Died of wound at Shiloh.
Babb John	Oct. 9, 1862.	Died Jan. 31, 1863, on board the hospital boat, Fanny Bullit.
Culp John* †	" 3, 1861.	Mustered out with the Regiment.
Colvin Reuben	" 3, "	Discharged in 1862, under age.
Colvin Edward	" 3, "	" "
Camp Frederick	" 3, "	Mustered out at expiration of term.
Cochran George	" 5, "	Died Aug. 21, 1863, on hospital boat, City of Memphis.
Chambers Edward	" 16, "	Died April 3, 1863, at Milliken's Bend, La.
Caldwell Mathew	" 23, "	Transferred to Co. H, Jan. 1, 1862.
Conrad Bartson	Dec. 6, "	" "
Carrier Alexander	Nov. 30, "	Died May 22, 1862, in hospital at St. Louis, Mo.
Campbell Jackson	July 14, 1862.	Discharged Dec. 9, 1862.
Dillon Peter*	Oct. 3, 1861.	" 1866.
Dermenier Etienne*	" 4, "	"
Dudley Campbell*	Nov. 30, "	Drowned in the Miss. river, June, 1864.
Eaglin William	Oct. 4, "	Died July 29, 1863, of camp fever, at Vicksburg.
Edgington David* †	Nov. 30, "	Mustered out with the Regiment.
Farris Lafayette	Oct. 3, "	Discharged under age in 1862.
Farris James M	" 3, "	Died May 24, 1862, near Corinth, Miss.
Farris W. S.	" 3, "	Died June 19, 1862, at home.
Gashett Sylvester	" 4, "	Died April 27, 1862, on hospital boat, Nashville.

Name	When Enlisted	
Haynor J. W.	Oct. 3, 1861.	Discharged July 16, 1862, at Cincinnati, O.
Hines Jacob *	" 3, "	Mustered out with the Regiment.
Hogan Thos.	" 3, "	Discharged Feb. 22, 1863, at Young's Point, La.
Hamontree John C.	" 3, "	Mortally wounded April 6, 1862. Died on his way to hospital.
Hess Anthony	" 3, "	Died May 11, 1862, at Cincinnati, O.
Harris Mason * †	" 3, "	Mustered out with the Regiment.
Holden John *	" 3, "	"
Hughey R. N.	" 6, "	Transferred to Co. H, Jan. 1, 1862.
Hays Warren M. †	" 3, "	Mustered out at expiration of term.
Hogan Daniel B.	Dec. 9, "	Wounded at Shiloh. Discharged Aug. 18, 1862, at St. Louis.
Hughey W. H. H.	" 14, "	Transferred to Co. H, Jan. 1, 1862
Jackson Jesse * †	Oct. 3, "	Mustered out with the Regiment.
Jones Ephraim *	" 4, "	Deserted at Houston, Texas, Feb, 1866.
Kellis Charles	Dec 27, "	Transferred to Co. H; discharged under age.
Kellis Amos	" 27, "	"
Lafferty William *	Oct. 10, "	Discharged 1865.
Laymon Amos	" 8, "	" Oct. 3, 1863, at New Orleans
Lafferty Elijah	" 6, "	" August 11, 1862, at Columbus, O.
Larkins John	" 3, "	" May, 1863, at Memphis, Tenn.
Lippolt Jacob	" 3, "	Mortally wounded April 6, 1862. Died at Louisville, Ky., April 28, 1862.
McDaniel D. R. * †	" 3, "	Mustered out with the Regiment.
McDaniel David	" 3, "	Discharged May, 1863, at Memphis.
Montgomery Samuel	" 3, "	Mustered out at expiration of term.
Marshall Enoch	" 3, "	Dropped from the rolls as deserter, Oct. 31, 1862.
Minzler John	" 5, "	Mustered out at expiration of term.
McCoy Alex	" 9, 1862.	Discharged Sept. 10, 1863, at Columbus, O.
Nelson Jesse	" 3, 1861.	Killed at the battle of Shiloh, April 6, 1862.
Newton Thomas H.	" 19, "	Mustered out at the close of the war.
Owens William	Dec. 27, "	Died Sept. 13, 1863, at Memphis.

Patton G. L.	Oct. 14, 1861.	" March 2, 1863, at Camp Dennison, O.
Pfister George	" 3, "	Wounded May 22, 1863. Discharged July 22, 1863, at St. Louis, Mo.
Pegan Thomas J	" 5, "	Transferred to Co. H. Discharged at expiration of term.
Pratt Jonathan	" 3, "	Mustered out at expiration of term.
Pemberton Russell	" 5, "	"
Pratt David R	" 4, "	"
Purdy James * †	Oct. 6, 1862.	Discharged June 16, 1862, at Lagrange, Tenn.
Raines Simpson	" 3, 1861.	Died in prison at Camp Ford, Texas, Aug. 1864. Mortally wounded at the battle of Shiloh; died on his way to the hospital.
Seal James †	" 3, "	Discharged in 1865.
Shafer Joshua * †	" 7, 1862.	Mustered out at expiration of original term.
Smith James S	" 3, 1861.	Transferred to Co. H, Jan. 1, 1862.
Stumbo James * †	" 3, "	Mustered out with Regiment.
Stumbo Joshua * †	" 11, "	"
Snider Peter	" 12, "	Died May 31, 1862, near Corinth, Miss.
Stronp William	" 12, 1862.	Discharged June 16, 1862, at Lagrange, Tenn.
Tedrick John H * †	" 12, "	Mustered out at expiration of original term.
Tedrick Morgan * †		"
Turnipseed Allen T. * †	" 3, 1861.	Promoted to Corporal; Wounded at Fort Blakely. Discharged 1865.
Thompson John H	" 14, "	Discharged June 21, 1863, at Vicksburg.
Thornburg Samuel	Feb. 1, 1862.	Dec. 9, 1862, at Memphis.
Vanpelt James	Oct. 4, 1861.	Wounded April 6, 1862. Discharged July 16, 1862, at Cincinnati, O.
Williams L. A	" 3, "	Mortally wounded May 22, 1862. Died May 27, 1862.
Workman Stephen	" 3, "	Transferred to Co. H, Jan. 1, 1862.
Workman Riley	" 3, "	"
Wood Riley	" 3, "	Discharged Dec 22, 1862.

Those marked * re-enlisted as Veterans.
Those marked † were taken prisoners at the battle of Sabine Cross-Roads, April 8th, 1864.

List of members of Co. C that have died since discharge from the service: Sergeants, Emanuel Kelso and J. D. Leonard; Privates, Patrick Boyland, J. W. Haynor, Amos Laymon and John Larkin.

The whole number of men enlisted in the Company was 108 (one hundred and eight). Of these:

12 Were transferred to Company H.
35 Discharged for disability, caused by wounds or disease.
11 Discharged by reason of expiration of their term.
15 Died of disease.
5 Died of wounds.
2 Killed in battle.
1 Drowned.
2 Deserted.
2 Promoted out of the Company.
5 Mustered out as supernumeraries.
14 Mustered out with the Regiment.
4 Officers resigned.

www.ingramcontent.com/pod-product-compliance
Lightning Source LLC
Chambersburg PA
CBHW022109230426
43672CB00008B/1321